THE E-HERO'S JOURNEY

THE E-HERO'S
JOURNEY

Your Guide to the Entrepreneur's Quest

BRANDON K. MOORE

The E-Hero's Journey:
Your Guide to the Entrepreneur's Quest
Copyright 2022, Brandon K. Moore

All rights reserved. No part of this publication may be reproduced or transmitted in any form or by any means, mechanical or electronic, including photocopying and recording, or by any information storage and retrieval system, without permission in writing from author (except by a reviewer, who may quote brief passages and/or show brief video clips in a review).

Disclaimer: The advice and strategies contained herein may not be suitable for your situation and should not replace the advice of a professional. If professional assistance is required, the services of a competent professional person should be sought. The author shall not be liable for damages arising herefrom.

ISBN (paperback): 978-1-5445-3060-4
ISBN (e-book): 978-1-5445-3061-1

*To Angela, my beautiful wife.
Thank you for being with me on this journey.*

*To Larry and Beth Lane, my beautiful wife's dad and mom.
I can't thank you enough for the impact you have had
on her, myself and my kids.*

CONTENTS

1. **Introduction to the Entrepreneur's Journey**   1

2. **The Dissatisfaction**   7
   Whether early in the journey or years after following the pack, every entrepreneur becomes dissatisfied with the status quo—and you will too.

3. **The Idea**   16
   Maybe there is a different way. An idea emerges—should I go out on my own and sell my product directly to the masses?

4. **The Choice**   25
   As dissatisfaction grows and the burning idea won't leave me alone, I draw a line in the sand that will change my life forever.

5. **The Call to Lead**   38
   Becoming an E-Hero is answering a call to lead others—vendors, customers, and employees. What type of leader am I now, and what kind of leader do I want to become?

6. **The Goal**   50
   My decision is made, and I see the goal. My vision defines my activities, driving me forward on my entrepreneur's journey.

7. **The Potential Unleashed**   63
   Results, feedback, and possibilities unleash my potential and cause me to tap the potential in others

8. **The Business Life Curve**   75
   Where am I? I assess where I am on the business life curve, which gives me insight into what comes next. I survey the potential obstacles ahead, which helps me prepare to meet them.

9. **The External Obstacles**   88
   I write my vision plainly, and I know my purpose. This holds me on course when I encounter obstacles seemingly at every turn.

10. The Internal Conflict   **103**

As pressure mounts, my character is tested. This battle within makes me question my original idea and choices.

11. The Win   **115**

Driving forward in a relentless pursuit of success, I meet the challenges of business head-on. Without claiming victory, I overcome and know that this entrepreneur life is the only life for me!

12. The Pitfalls of Success   **125**

Success brings potential pitfalls. I learn hard lessons that teach me to beware of pride, fear, and vanity.

13. The Better Life   **135**

On the other side of victory, I realize I have grown up as a person and business leader. There are still challenges ahead, but I have overcome them before, and I will overcome them again.

14. The Conclusion   **144**

Appendix: You Should Read List   **155**

About the Author   **159**

CHAPTER 1

INTRODUCTION TO THE ENTREPRENEUR'S JOURNEY

On July 8, 2004, I woke up extra early. I donned my best suit and tie. My freshly shined shoes glinted in the sun. After my morning coffee, my wife and I drove together to sign the paperwork to purchase my first CPA firm. A local band was playing outside, and several food trucks had gathered to help us celebrate. As we entered the building, the previous owner, Ron Lentz, welcomed me with a big smile and hearty handshake. After we signed, he announced to the crowd that I was the new top Certified Public Accountant (CPA) in town! The mayor cut a ribbon with giant scissors as the people cheered. My friends and family had gathered and were all so proud. Once I signed those papers, I knew my life had changed!

None of that really happened.

Honestly, I don't remember much about that day. To have so much significance in my life, you would think I would remember more. Mostly I recall being nervous about signing the asset purchase agreement and handing over a significant check to Ron. The newly created debt with virtually no collateral was a huge weight.

After I signed, I just went to work. No, my wife, Angela, didn't come with me to witness this great event. No crowd gathered, no band played, no announcement was made. Not at "the event"—not even a byline in the newspaper or anywhere else for that matter. The most fanfare we managed was sending letters to the clients inviting them to meet me and informing them of Ron's retirement.

Funny thing, I wasn't nervous anymore. Once the deal was done, I became the entrepreneur I was meant to be. It was a monumental day, one that changed our lives completely. But it was a personal victory. One that I have thanked God for many times.

If you have read many novels, taken creative writing courses, or studied filmmaking, you know about The Hero's Journey. It is the basis for almost all works of fiction. Think Luke Skywalker in *Star Wars* or Neo in *The Matrix*. The hero's journey begins with an ordinary person shaken out of his everyday life. A need arises, and he chooses to go on a quest. Sometimes the quest is for justice, sometimes out of necessity, and sometimes motivated by pain. No matter, he must choose to go. He will face insurmountable obstacles and must confront the need to make a change within himself. Ultimately, he grows, defeats an enemy, completes a nearly impossible task, wins the object of his quest, and comes out victorious on the other side. He is now a different, better version of himself.

Successful entrepreneurs go through a process that parallels the hero's journey. This book is from one Entrepreneur Hero (E-Hero) to another. It contains the advice and experience I wish I could have had when I began my quest.

The reality of the pain, blood, sweat, and tears of the E-Hero's Journey was always there around me, but it was hidden in books or veiled in the theory and academic advice of others. Without question, the E-Hero's journey is best understood by experience.

So why am I writing this book then?

I hope to inspire you. I hope to warn you. <u>E-Heros who go it alone rarely succeed</u>. Accepting counsel and walking in the footsteps of those who have gone before, all while innovating and carving out new and creative paths, is the entrepreneur's ultimate opportunity. The journey isn't for everyone, but maybe it's for you.

In *Indiana Jones and The Last Crusade*, Indy could navigate the obstacles and obtain the prize only because he was given clues that helped him through three impossible trials. They were clues, not answers. He had to figure out how they applied and choose what to do with them, but the advice was critical to his success. This book gives you those clues to overcome the obstacles you will face ahead.

> The journey isn't for everyone, but maybe it's for you.

What You Will Learn

From this book, you will learn what motivates the E-Hero's journey. You'll recognize the dissatisfaction with the status quo (or life as the entrepreneur knows it). We'll talk about how the idea begins, is fleshed out, and evaluated. You'll make a choice, knowing there are consequences to every choice and costs for every quest. How will you do things differently? Will you start a business or change a department process? Once you choose, you must fix your vision.

You will learn to write and record your goal and that all activities and strategies must align with that goal. Along the way, you, the E-Hero, will encounter obstacles. Those must be faced and overcome. Both external and internal. You will meet external challenges with creativity and recognize internal conflicts as growth opportunities. The climax of the E-Hero's journey is the big win. We'll discover what an entrepreneur's win is and celebrate all the big and small victories along the way.

And on the other side of the big win, you'll experience a better life. Not without continued challenges, not without being wary of the pitfalls of success, but a better life awaits you all the same.

About the Author

I help people and businesses succeed. I am a Certified Public Accountant (CPA) and Financial Advisor with a CPA firm I established in 2004. Actually, I have three companies with multiple revenue streams.

Before buying the firm from a retiring CPA, I began buying rental real estate. I have more than eighty single-family residences and a handful of duplexes as I write this book.

I also have a financial services company with three other financial advisors in our group. For more than twenty years, I have been in business for myself and worked with other small businesses.

The E-Hero's journey is birthed from my passion for helping entrepreneurs and those with an entrepreneurial spirit to succeed. I hope you will be inspired and directed towards a better life for yourself and your family. Living life with passion and purpose is much more fulfilling than just having a job. I want that for you. With all my heart, I want that for you.

What You Should Do Next

Read this book for you. Let it spark your entrepreneurial potential. Unless you are excited to the bone about human resources, engineering, statistical analysis, banking, finance, or whatever your chosen field, it is difficult to be passionate about the pre-defined career path.

Many are dissatisfied with their jobs. We now have fewer people staying at their company for more than three years, indicating restlessness. Many of my clients have had several career changes until they found one that suits them. Some are in different fields than they studied in college. That is okay. What

> Living life with passion and purpose is much more fulfilling than just having a job.

isn't okay is being in a job for years and feeling stuck. Because you might do well or have a talent for the job, you think you have no options and have no hope for a change. This book will give you ideas on how to change that.

So, without any more delay, let's get right into the E-Hero's Journey!

CHAPTER 2

THE DISSATISFACTION

We open the scene with you, the hero, reflecting on your current world. A world with rules and regulations. A world where everyone expects you to behave a certain way, show up at a certain time and answer to a certain employer. Though it seems normal at first, the day-to-day grind of activities slowly kills you from the inside. The pressure mounts until some catalyst awakens you, and you know that stasis equals death! If something doesn't change, if you don't go on this journey, it could be catastrophic for everyone.

That seems a little dramatic, I know. But calling on the parallels of a fiction novel helps set the stage for the dissatisfaction that all entrepreneurs feel with the way things are done. The way they are supposed to behave. People pressure you to fit into their box and abide by their rules! But you, the E-Hero, see through that mist and reach out for something more.

I remember when my daughter, Kate, was a senior in high school, and all the teachers were telling her she needed to get dual credit; she needed to have obtained this score on the SAT/

ACT by this date; fill out her financial aid forms by this date, or she was behind schedule! "Don't get left behind!" "This is the way to do it!" "Trust us; we know what we are saying!"

Those teachers knew (or think they knew) the way—the one and only way. But the truth about life is that there are many ways to succeed. If you interview the most successful people in any town or the heads of fortune 500 companies, few will have similar stories. Some went into the military, some worked for years in the oil and gas industry, some started their own business right after high school, and yes, some will have gone to college and found success.

The high school Kate was in boasted a 98% college acceptance rate at the time. They didn't go any further, though. They considered themselves successful if they got those young adults to the steps of the university. But what happens so many times after that is just sad. A lot of wasted money and time later, many young people drop out. It wasn't for them, or they had chosen a field at age 18 they knew little about and learned they either didn't like it or weren't that good at it.

High schools put *so* much pressure on kids that, similar to Kate's school, many were on anti-depressants, in therapy, or just gave up on life. Did I mention that the way things are is just sad?

I recently had a conversation with a counselor about how many hours of high school credits you have to have to apply to college in Texas. They swore it was twenty-six, which is how many you earn if you are in the accelerated program for most schools. I got off the phone and called two separate state schools and asked them about this so-called "requirement." They had no such requirement for admittance. All the counselor had to do to find out was make a few phone calls herself. The truth is, many teachers and counselors barely know what they are pushing, much less about how to be successful in life.

I am not knocking educators. We need them. But our educational system is out of touch with all but one well-defined, deeply engrained idea of how to prepare for a career. It has not been updated or broadened its scope to take in the rapidly changing opportunities, technology, and business models of our time.

So, if good grades and a traditional college degree are not the only way, then how do you become successful in life? Later we will define what success means. In the dissatisfaction stage, E-Heroes begin the journey to search for another way.

It is Inevitable.

If it hasn't happened to you yet, it will eventually. Whether you are just starting out or have been around a while, the dissatisfaction will creep in. The story begins the same every day. While weekends give you some repose, they too will become dissatisfying. Looking like every other day, Monday will cause you anxiety just thinking about it. Your alarm goes off; you work out for a bit, shower, and go to work, either at the office or at home. It doesn't matter. You get to work, say hi to the same people, make your morning cup of whatever and sit down in your designated work area. "God," you wonder, "is it 5 o'clock yet? I know I just got here, but damn!"

You used to be creative. Remember that? Maybe it was third grade, but it was there. Now, look at you. You are not only dissatisfied, but you are also disgusted with yourself. No, not with yourself—with this desk, these pencils, the monitor, and the phone—all a constant bother. You worked so hard to get there, college or trade school or maybe just the training months. You thought that this job was what you wanted.

You may not know this, but you are not alone. Countless thousands of people are there or have been there before. You may not be aware, but you have been trained to think very linearly. Point A to point B, straight line. You were told in high school that you need to get a good-paying job to be successful. To get a good-paying job, you should go to college, trade school, or a training program to be a police officer or fireman. That is a melting pot of mediocrity. A dream stealer built into our education system and no more built on reality than Hogwarts.

We no longer encourage young people to explore their interests. Discover who they are. We expect that to happen at college. That's expensive therapy. My wife and I encouraged our kids to find jobs after high school that interested them. If that was indeed an area they wanted to continue in, and college was necessary to do it, then we would help them make that happen. There's no use sending an 18-year-old to college if they don't have a clue what they want to do.

Many of my clients started in one career and discovered that they really liked something else better. Of the financial advisors that I know, only a handful have a finance degree. Many were teachers, pastors, worked in agriculture or some other vocation before realizing what they could be passionate about.

Who's to Blame?

The dissatisfaction comes especially to those who follow someone else's career plan. Parents are to blame here, and I am not excluding myself. I had dreams of my boys playing for a Major League Baseball team or my daughter becoming a real estate attorney (it could still happen). If others have pushed you down a career path that was not a fit for you, I'm sorry. Really sorry. The desire to please our parents and be affirmed by those we love can be a powerful driving force—for good or evil. And if we choose a career that sucks the soul right out of us, dissatisfaction is going to emerge.

Now that some of my kids are out of high school, I won't tell them what I think they should do unless they ask. It is a hard transition to make. Going from telling them what to do every moment of the day to only advising is a giant leap. If you have kids, I recommend you start early. Stop making all the decisions for them when they are around 14 or so, and give them some opportunities to try and fail.

If you were parented this way and all your choices were made for you, then today is the perfect time to wean yourself from abdicating decisions to others or blaming where you are today on how you were raised. You are in charge of your future.

My wife and I firmly believe in raising our kids to be adults and training them accordingly. Many parents aren't preparing their kids to be adults. They don't know it, but they're training their kids to be kids. Early in life, our kids learn decision-making; it's one of those "adulting" areas. I haven't liked some of my kid's decisions, but that doesn't mean I'll take back the responsibility from them.

When my son Ian was between twelve and fourteen years old, every time we went to a restaurant, he ordered something he didn't like. It happened so often that he asked me to choose for him. I said, "I won't order for you, but I will make a recommendation for what I believe you will like." That worked. He was happy, I didn't pay for something that he wouldn't eat, and the decision was still his.

Wildness Lost

Life tends to tame the wildness that should be alive in all of us. When I say wildness, I don't mean rebellion. I mean that passion needs to be allowed to run free and see what can happen. We are not always supposed to conform. We should release and explore the creativity in our lives. Without the release, we get dissatisfied with life. With the standard career path, there is little expression of self.

What makes a relationship with your spouse so satisfying is the passion. The intimacy of each other's souls being completely open and vulnerable. True, it isn't like it appears in books or movies, although I dig the romantic chic flick.

> Life tends to tame the wildness that should be alive in all of us.

(Don't tell anyone, or I will totally lose my man card.) But passion is more than heat; it is longing and satisfaction from a deep relationship.

How does that compare to your career? Well, it isn't completely insane to think you can experience passion in your work. Especially when you put everything on the line for something you believe in and enjoy. A young lady once told me that she took a job in a manufacturing company. I asked her how that was. "I absolutely love it!" she said. I was shocked. "I could never be passionate about the products," she continued, "but the challenge and my team make the job extremely rewarding."

Where Does It Lead?

Dissatisfaction leads to many places. It can lead to resentment and bitterness, blaming everyone else for your status in life. This kind of dissatisfaction usually causes change in a negative way. A boss sees how you interact with the team and decides he doesn't want that kind of negative energy. You feel boxed in. Angry. So you explode at your team or boss and walk away from your job. Think about the times you have been disappointed with life and, like a pressure cooker, you just let it all out. We've all done this. It doesn't end well. Bridges are burned, relationships are broken, and it takes a while to pick up the pieces.

When I was sixteen, I worked at a Sonic after school and on weekends. For those of you who may not know what a Sonic is, it's a drive-up burger joint where servers are sometimes on roller skates to take the food to the cars. My manager was a guy named Harry who obviously didn't like people. He motivated the staff by yelling, screaming, and slamming things down on the prep tables. It was awful. The only thing I liked about working there was one of the stunningly gorgeous carhops. She would take and fill orders from the customers and, in between orders, sing hits from musicals. She must have been in the theater arts program at the local university. I would have listened to her sing all day if I could.

One day an order was placed and somehow got lost in the shuffle. It took longer than the target 5 minutes to deliver, so Harry became unleashed. That insanity was directed at me. I had had enough. After his rant subsided, I took a tape from the register and wrote, "Harry, I quit! Brandon." Then I put it on the ledge where we lined up orders for prep. I wanted it to look like an incomplete order. Then, I walked out the back door without a word. I left that beautiful songbird behind. She wasn't enough to make me want to stay. Later I found out Harry looked at the tape and, before reading it, started yelling at everyone for missing an order. He nearly busted a vein when he picked up the paper to read it.

I got a little too much enjoyment from that. I was so unhappy that I blew up that bridge and walked away. Why? Dissatisfaction.

Where else can dissatisfaction lead? Boredom, monotony. A life of regret and loss of zest for life. It can lead to nowhere. Dissatisfaction *is* the road to nowhere. People who take this road are lost and without hope of change. I have never really been this person, so I don't understand it well, but I have seen it often enough.

We have all heard the definition of insanity; doing the same thing over and over and expecting a different result. When people do something repeatedly without any expectation at all, they are not interested in change. Maybe because change scares them? Perhaps because they think it will rock the boat and they like a stable boat? Another cliché is that "the only thing that is constant is change." Sometimes these folks go out of their way to prove that wrong.

Time for Change

Where *should* dissatisfaction lead? You guessed it. Change—the beginning of the E-Hero's journey. It must happen that way. If there is no dissatisfaction, any entrepreneur's journey will quickly end and resort back to the way things were. No one wants negative change; you want positive change. Creativity moves you past dissatisfaction in a responsive, non-reactionary way.

There's a story about an old farmer and his dog. The man and canine were sitting on the porch when a stranger came calling. The dog wailed in pain every few seconds, shifted his weight, and lay back down. The stranger asked, "Why does he keep wailing like that?"

The farmer replied, "There's a nail on the porch underneath him that hurts him when he lies down."

The stranger asked, "Why doesn't he move?"

"It doesn't hurt enough for him to want to move." The farmer replied.

> Creativity moves you past dissatisfaction in a responsive, non-reactionary way.

When your dissatisfaction hurts enough, you will move. And with that, we are on to the next chapter, The Idea.

The Dissatisfaction—Chapter Summary

- Dissatisfaction happens to everyone at some point in their lives.
- You shouldn't trade your wildness, passion, and creativity for a job.
- Dissatisfaction causes you either to burn bridges or build new ones.
- Dissatisfaction should lead you to change: change yourself, change your career, change the way you think about life.
- Dissatisfaction may be the catalyst you need to start your E-Hero's journey.

CHAPTER 3

THE IDEA

Your E-Hero journey is well underway. Now that your world has unraveled and the dissatisfaction is so overwhelming, you must fashion a plan. You must either discover a possible solution or identify an escape route. The status quo is no longer a viable option. When Luke Skywalker finds Obi-Wan (or is found by Obi), they both fall back to Obi's hideout, listen to the hidden message from Princess Lea and discuss what must inevitably come next. They need an idea, a hopeful plan for the future. Before you leave your old world behind, E-Hero, you need an idea.

There are no great ideas.

What? How can I possibly say such a thing?

Indeed we have seen some great ideas in the last two centuries that brought us out of agricultural-based economies, through the industrial revolution, and into the technological advancement of the late 20th century. Didn't Solomon say there is nothing new under the sun?

Obviously, there has been a lot of new stuff? We know Solomon wasn't talking about stuff. He was talking about seasons, relationships, people, and ideas. So back to my original statement—there are no great ideas. There are only ideas, and we choose to make them great.

I completely stole that. I read Sean Platt and Johnny B. Truant's *The Fiction Formula, The New Rules For Self Publishing Success,* and was inspired by their discussion about coming up with great book ideas. They don't exist. What stirs our dissatisfaction is a need for change. The journey begins in the mind with rationalizing risk and analysis of costs. Like the founders of the Sony corporation, E-Heroes know they want to go into business for themselves. The type of business or the product you sell is irrelevant at this stage. Developing the HOW isn't required right now as much as the WHY. In your mind, a conversation happens:

> The journey begins in the mind with rationalizing risk and analysis of costs.

Q: Why am I unhappy?
A: Because I hate my job,
Q: Why do I hate my job?
A: Because it doesn't satisfy me.
Q: Why does it not satisfy you?
Q: Why are you asking so many questions? Are my lips moving? Are people watching?

The questioning is essential. It will help you discover what you are looking to get out of a new career, business venture, or just a job change. If you just want to "make more money," you really need to keep digging. Why do you want to make more money? Do you have other plans, investments, or a family to provide for or spend more time doing "X" (not the drug, by the way)? Anyway, this WHY needs to be settled in your heart, or you won't withstand what comes later—the internal and external obstacles. "Making more money" as your WHY may create ethical crossroads down the line. If that is your only motivation, you will hurt people along the way to get there, including yourself. Then you are no longer the hero of this story; YOU ARE THE VILLAIN!

Love of Money

Money is **not** the root of all evil; the *love* of money is the root of all evil. Money that has purpose is a virtuous endeavor and should be celebrated and encouraged. Robert Kiyosaki, in his book *Rich Dad, Poor Dad, What The Rich Teach Their Kids About Money That The Poor Do Not*, talks about the value of giving. Generosity is an excellent motivation for change. To give more, you have to have more than enough for yourself and your family. Dissatisfaction is uncomfortable, but if it leads you to ask these questions, then it is doing its job.

My family's values are rooted in generosity. I love to provide for my kids, give gifts to my wife, give to our church and the community. It is one of the joys of my life and the real purpose for pushing forward. After reaching many work and investment goals, we could have sat back and relaxed in all that God has blessed us with. I chose to press on, make new goals, and continue to learn and grow in my leadership. Why? Because there are more gifts to give, more people to hire and develop into professionals, more churches to plant, more dogs to rescue, and more causes to support.

So get your WHY worked out.

Once you have your WHY in mind, you now need that idea to bring about the change you crave. I said before that there are no great ideas, but that doesn't mean you shouldn't have big ideas. Big has two meanings here. One is that it is high-level and overarching. It shouldn't be too specific right now; the details will come later. Answer the statement, "I think I would like to _____." Or, "I think I would like to become a(n) _____." Just something to start with, pointing you in a general direction. Your career path may resemble more of the flight of a butterfly here than a train on a track. Honestly, your ideas can evolve over time, getting more and more specific as your understanding of the industry changes or the development of the business you created grows. The Bible offers great advice: "Do not despise small beginnings."[1] Small beginnings start with big ideas.

The second meaning of a "big" idea is that it has room for growth. If there is no room for growth, you will end up back in the dissatisfaction stage. How scalable is your idea? Even if it is a taco stand, can you replicate it and grow it into a fleet of taco stands? No one should dream of becoming something small. Ray Croc, the founder of McDonald's, took a small burger place in San Bernadino, California, and with a system he could replicate, he built an empire. It is acceptable for kids to believe that a lemonade stand is a big idea venture as an entrepreneur, but not for grown-ups. Allow yourself to dream here. Dream of what is possible.

---

1   Zechariah 4:10.

Dream Stealers

Dream stealers are the doubts and fears of people in your inner circle who would criticize you for dreaming but who have never done anything of value. Be careful of these. Stay away from those people; stay away from those thoughts. In the idea stage, thinking too much about the HOW can bog you down and discourage you. HOW (for now) is unnecessary.

    I am not talking about dreaming of fame and fortune or winning Grammys for debut albums—*especially* if you can't sing. Dreaming big is not dreaming the impossible. No, I am talking about letting your heart believe the things that are possible and keeping your mind from interrupting that flow with fear and doubt. For example, I was told I would not pass the CPA exam the first time. I told everyone who would listen that I would. Not out of arrogance, but out of a belief that I could and knowing that it was possible if I worked hard enough. The more people I told, the more I reinforced that belief and made myself accountable.

    What kinds of ideas are possible but are still big ideas?

    That is a great question! Starting a business, becoming an author, investing in real estate, starting a church or non-profit; these are all big ideas. Other ideas like becoming an engineer, a CPA, an attorney, or a medical doctor are also in the big idea vein but have a more prescribed vocational path. That's okay. I don't believe that the entrepreneurial spirit is limited to those who are self-employed. You can be the head of a crew or department, division manager, a leader in a Fortune 500 company, manager of a small business, or an on-call physician and still be an E-Hero!

Entrepreneurial Spirit

What is the entrepreneurial spirit? It is hard to define. If you search for it on the internet, you will find several articles that list words like passion, determination, leadership, innovation, fearlessness, etc. Since the definition depends on the author, I will do my best to take a shot at it. A person with an entrepreneurial spirit is a curious individual who loves to ask why not and which way forward from here. They do have ambition, but it isn't selfish. They have a healthy respect for the possibility of failure but do not let it keep them from trying.

Risk-taking always happens after calculating the potential losses and gains, and then deciding that the gains are worth it. The phrase "Work smarter, not harder" isn't necessarily true. The E-Hero works hard at smart work; they don't want to waste time working in ignorance. The one thing the entrepreneur has that others don't is vision. Vision is the almost prophetic understanding of how things can be if other things are done and done well. The entrepreneur may get frustrated because the vision is so clear to them, in full color in their mind's eye, they genuinely don't understand how you can't see it. Entrepreneurs love freedom—freedom to make decisions, run with their ideas, and receive the rewards from the results.

> A person with an entrepreneurial spirit is a curious individual who loves to ask why not and which way forward from here.

Diving into the Details

Once you have the idea and can clearly articulate what that idea is, it is time to start fleshing out the details. Write the idea down on the middle of a blank piece of paper or whiteboard. Then, create a mind map with strategies around it. For example, you might put "start a business" in the middle, then write types of businesses all around it. When doing this, start with industries that you know something about or that really interest you. Understand that for industries you don't know anything about, you will have to do some research before moving forward. The business you start doesn't have to be an original "mom and pop" shop; it could be a franchise or national chain that offers local ownership.

Once you have a pretty good map, circle two or three of the best choices, the ones that are most likely to happen. Then start the process over with each potential choice, this time getting more detailed as to what must happen to create that business. The goal is to start very broad and get increasingly more detailed at each level. For instance, you write down "owning a postal service type franchise" (several of these brands are available as franchises). Then you write around it financing, staffing, locations, creating an LLC, and other things. From that list, pick two or three that must be done first and create an action plan.

The action plan is a great way to put feet to your idea. Since it is still an idea, you can play around with this process several times with several different possible business ideas or vocational choices before committing any resources. Your action plan should have start dates and due dates for each action, though I probably wouldn't fill in the actual dates just yet. Not until you have hammered out which idea, strategies, and activities you are going to do. What I would do next is pray. I am a person of faith, so I would never even think of setting off on a journey without talking to the Wonderful Counselor who holds my future in His hands.[2]

If that isn't for you, consider talking to some counselors (they won't be as wonderful). By the way, that is also what I would do next. I have learned the value of feedback and wise counsel. Get feedback from people who know you, know your strengths and weaknesses, and, most importantly, understand your chosen industry. This will probably include several different people, and that's okay. In fact, it's better.[3]

Remember before when I said be careful to avoid dream stealers? Well, sometimes good counsel sounds like dream stealing. Sometimes you flesh out an idea but don't know anything about the industry or tactics necessary to succeed. Good counsel should make you aware of any blind spots. Don't be discouraged. Figure out what you can do to mitigate those blind spots.

When I looked to increase the number of advisors in our financial services group, I was told to get a supervisory license first. I wasn't excited about getting that license because then I would be responsible for monitoring the other advisors and doing more paperwork. Yuck! So instead, I talked it over with some people who knew more about the process, and we came up with an alternative, and the dream is still alive!

Good counsel from other business owners, CPAs, or attorneys is always a good idea. The difference between good

---

2   Psalm 31.
3   Proverbs 11:14.

counsel and dream stealing is whether their advice is intended to encourage or discourage you. Someone pointing out obstacles and pitfalls before you encounter them is priceless. Wise counsel will save you time, money, and heartache.

Okay, E-Hero, now you have an idea for a business, and just like Luke Skywalker had to make a choice, you have to decide what to do with that big, beautiful idea.

The Idea - Chapter Summary

- There are no great ideas. You make your idea great.
- Determine the WHY behind your idea.
- Answer the statement, "I think I would like to _____." Or, "I think I would like to become a(n) _____."
- Does your idea have room for growth? Is it scalable now? Will it continue to be scalable?
- Be careful of dream stealers—the doubts and fears of people in your inner circle who would criticize you for dreaming but who have never done anything of value.
- If you are a curious individual who loves to ask why not and which way forward from here, you have an entrepreneurial spirit.
- Mindmap your idea(s) and select those most likely to get done. Then mindmap the next steps for each of those ideas.
- Seek good counsel from those who know what you have not yet learned.

CHAPTER 4

THE CHOICE

One of the greatest choice moments in cinematic history came during the first movie of the *Matrix Trilogy*, released in 1999 by the Wachowski brothers. Neo, played by Keanu Reeves, follows the white rabbit into the company of Trinity and, ultimately, the man he has been searching for, Morpheus. In this scene, before Neo can understand the Matrix, he must first choose to continue searching or go back to his old life.

Can you imagine being Neo in that chair as Morpheus opens his hands in front of him, revealing two pills? Take the red pill, and his mind will be opened to the truth, and he will enter a new world. Take the blue pill, and he will wake up back in his apartment, reinstalled into the old world. The caveat; once you take the red pill, you can never go back.

Fortunately, your E-Hero decision has fewer epic consequences. But there are consequences. Failure is possible. Failure in business could result in ruined credit, loss of savings, and sleeping on your parents' couch. But success is also possible, and your entrepreneur dreams can lead to great fulfillment.

This chapter will discuss that decision—the choice—and the costs associated with it.

Choosing Self-Employment

Choosing to go out on your own is a tough decision. Even if you have partners or a spouse to help you, it is still a hard choice. On the one hand, you could be an employee, working for someone else from nine to five. On the other, you could be your own boss and never work from nine to five again.

Before making that choice, you need to understand your decision (that may be a *Matrix* reference). Each decision has its risks and rewards. Many are not cut out to be self-employed. They have always been and probably always will be an employee. There is nothing wrong with that. It is not inherently better or worse than being self-employed; it is just a different path.

If you are an entrepreneur employee, as discussed in the next section, you can have a lasting impact as a member of a team or department working for someone else. We will talk more about this avenue of an E-Hero's journey later. For now, let's get into the choice of making it on your own.

Organizational Chart of One

Remember when I said you would never have a nine-to-five job again? That's because in the beginning stages of a business, you are there before everyone else and leave much later. It isn't because self-employed people are workaholics, but because there is so much to do!

Every startup has many seats at the table, but they may all be filled by the same person—you! For example, when you start the business, you might think of yourself as a salesperson, a mechanic, a CPA (myself included), but you will quickly find out that you are also the CEO, CFO, accounting manager, customer service desk, and every other role that you haven't hired yet.

It is up to you to get these jobs done until you grow and hire to fill those seats. Some businesses never grow because the owner doesn't want to release control of those jobs. Others are fine with releasing them but don't oversee them well to ensure the person hired truly represents the business.

When you choose to launch out on your own, you need to know that it won't just be about your industry and your work, but also all the little things that different departments at large companies do will rest on your shoulders.

Risk of One Employer

You should also consider the risk of making a profit versus the stability of working as an employee. During an interview for school, my daughter asked me why I decided to buy a CPA firm instead of taking a job at a multi-partner firm. You can hear that interview on my *Coaching For Profit* podcast, available on Spotify, Youtube, and other podcasts platforms. It wasn't an easy decision, but my job history preceding my decision made it the only alternative.

I had been laid off or fired four times in the previous ten years. Truthfully, one of those was my fault; the rest had nothing to do with me. Each time I had felt helpless and without control of my life. The first time it happened, I had just gotten married. My boss had hired me as the receptionist for his insurance agency. The bi-lingual person he hired was having trouble passing the licensing test, so he offered me a small raise if I would take and pass it. Two license tests later, I was a property and casualty insurance solicitor and a life, accident, and health insurance agent.

After several months, and now a newlywed, my boss's son-in-law was let go at an agency in a nearby town. My boss reluctantly said he couldn't afford to have both of us. I was let go. It was a horrible feeling of loss, uncertainty, and failure. I didn't know what to do but go home and tell Angela, my wife. Thankfully, I have never stayed unemployed very long. Opportunities found their way to my door, and food was always on the table. But you do not forget those feelings.

The last time I was laid off was when I worked for Arthur Andersen. It was one of the top 5 accounting firms in the country, with eighty thousand employees worldwide. It felt secure … until a company named Enron went belly-up. Andersen was the audit company engaged to work on verifying their financial statements. I have opinions on why the firm went under when many other firms have had worse audit failures and are still breathing. But for this story, just know that I was devastated. I had moved my family, my wife and our two oldest kids, from West Texas to Irving, Texas, for this job. You would think a company that had been in existence for eighty years was pretty stable. Well, you and I would be wrong.

All this happened shortly after September 11, 2001. On that day, working in the tallest building in Dallas, I had to evacuate the building with my co-workers down fifty-six flights of stairs. Many had already begun losing their jobs with the chaos that followed. Then, Enron was the focus of every news cycle for months. It was tough to stay focused on work when everyone's minds were full of fear and anxiety. In the spring of 2002, the HR department called me into their office. Again, I was let go. Most of my colleagues walked across the street to Deloitte, KPMG, or other top four accounting firms. KPMG actually had interviews in our offices for anyone who wanted to sign up, and most were eventually hired. I found work within a few weeks back in San Angelo, TX. The partners and managers who had to stay to finish the audits they were working on got the worst of it. After Andersen lost its firm license in Texas, those audits were ultimately ignored and redone by other companies. Those were the two most dramatic layoffs I experienced.

Afterward, back in West Texas, a solo CPA practice hired me. Though brilliant, he had some character issues. He wanted me to buy into his firm, even going as far as legally adding my name to the firm. Looking into his practice as a potential shareholder uncovered many problems. One was that he hadn't done his own tax return in several years. Usually, when you buy a business, you request the tax returns to get an idea of the reported revenues and expenses as well as outstanding debt. People might inflate a balance sheet or their profit and loss to make them look good. But the numbers they report to the IRS are not likely to be inflated. Since he hadn't filed in so many years, I determined that he was either hiding something or was irresponsible. Either way, it was a big turn-off in the relationship.

Also, I didn't like some of the ways he served the clients. I don't want to say here what that was, but it just didn't feel right. People tell you to observe how your potential spouse treats their parents; it gives you an idea of your impending marriage. Observe your potential partners the same way. I saw some things that made me want to look elsewhere. When I told him I no longer wanted to buy in, he responded by making me a contractor instead of an employee. In my mind, that was the same as being fired.

Our relationship was a bit contentious after that. I could feel him trying to push me out. So, when the opportunity came to purchase a firm and be my own boss, I felt like that was the best choice.

As an employee, you have many risks that self-employed people don't have. In the months of the COVID-19 lockdowns, many found out how risky being an employee can be. All occupations involve some amount of risk. You are an E-Hero. You don't shy away from risk; you manage it through preparation and education.

> As an employee, you have many risks that self-employed people don't have.

What The Choice Means

I didn't want to be subject to another layoff. Now, instead of having one employer, I have over one thousand. If one chooses to let me go, it doesn't mean I have lost my livelihood. To me, that is job security. That may comfort some, and to others, it may be even more stressful. Having so many "employers" also means that you have one thousand people telling you what to do.

It really shouldn't take one minute of sleep from you to be self-employed. As a self-employed E-Hero, you get to choose who you serve. At our firm, we decide what clients we want to work with. Occasionally, a client has issues with us, and we work them out. For the most part, we partner with our clients to help them reach their goals.

New Financial World

When you consider being self-employed, you need to understand that it will affect your whole financial world. Borrowing money for a home will be more complicated. How you pay taxes on your income is now very different.

People pay me thousands of dollars per year to figure out how their businesses can be structured just to pay less taxes. Retirement planning becomes a bit more complicated, sometimes better for the self-employed, yet still complicated. All of this can be managed with good advisors and a focus on continuous self-improvement. You are your best advisor.

I'm not saying that you shouldn't have a CPA, attorney, banker, and business coach. I am saying that you should take the time to understand your industry and strive to be the best at it. That happens through reading, classes, or industry education. Learning should never stop for the entrepreneur.

The Entrepreneur Employee

The entrepreneur employee is rare, but they are out there. Usually, they are in industries or businesses they believe in. They are the ones who get promoted first and are ambitious for the company's mission! Any employee at any level can choose to become this person. When you decide to give yourself to the position, you connect with the company and know that your part plays a role in the company's success.

Entrepreneur employees aren't motivated by financial incentives alone. Yes, compensation is important, and high-performing employees should be rewarded accordingly. But motivation doesn't come from being paid more. Being paid more is a result of motivation. What motivates an entrepreneur employee is the challenge itself!

Challenge yourself by setting big hairy audacious goals (BHAGs) and working diligently to accomplish them. The E-Hero employee aligns their goals with the company's goals. For example, BKM pc CPAs wants to be our clients' most trusted advisor. Our employees align their goals by focusing their professional development towards business advisory, tax planning, and business coaching methods. Those employees who don't have these goals will find it hard to succeed in our organization.

An E-Hero employee is happy only with an employer who has spent a good amount of time and energy forming the company's vision and core values. They want to work for employers who set BHAGs, not only for the executive team but also to motivate employees. Entrepreneur employees cannot engage if their organization does not have clarity of purpose and vision for the future.

If you believe you are an entrepreneur employee with high expectations and drive but are at a company lost at sea without a compass, you may need to find another employer. Or, if you are in a position to inspire change, put all your efforts into helping create clarity for the company. If possible, help the company leaders see their need for a clear vision. Ask them to define the core values, purpose, and long-term goals.

Motivation comes from clarity in these areas.

If you are the business owner, paying attention to these things helps you identify who belongs and who may need to find other employment. Those who share the company's values and want to be a part of the mission will thrive, while those who don't will leave or show you why they need to be let go.

Counting the Costs

Before you make the choice to set out on the entrepreneur journey, you must count the costs. As an advisor to clients and an entrepreneur myself, I know that when we look at the costs of an enterprise, we tend to round down. Like my wife, when she reports how much she spent shopping, we tend to be more optimistic about what revenues may come in, the market demand for our product, or the ease of attracting new customers. It is imperative that you look at the cold hard facts *and* maintain your entrepreneurial spirit that still says, "We can do this!" You should be prepared for all the difficulty that this road promises, but remember that you are the hero of this story.

> Before you make the choice to set out on the entrepreneur journey, you must count the costs.

This book doesn't contain spreadsheets and graphs. (I do love spreadsheets, though.) I don't need to show you a chart for you to learn that you should expect things to cost more than your estimates and that your employees won't immediately believe in the mission. A saying that applies here is, "Expect the best, prepare for the worst." You can't prepare for everything, but you can prepare for some things. You can estimate a 20% growth rate in the first three years but prepare for 0-6% growth. Or even negative growth. Sometimes sales are seasonal.

    Count the cost. Prepare.

    As a new business owner, you may not be familiar with the seasons of the industry. You may be flush with cash and feel wealthy, then later that year, or the next year, have a considerable shortage. I once worked with a Realtor who had a great year. I warned him about the seasonality and ups and downs of the real estate market, but he quickly went out and bought a new house and a Cadillac. Did he fund his retirement plan? No. Did he save anything for his taxes due the following year? No. I told him, "Well, you spent your tax money on that car, and I guess you will retire on the gain from selling your house?"

    You don't know what you don't know. You can prepare for contingencies but not for every possible contingency. So what are the costs you should focus on counting? I am glad you asked. There are several you should consider. The main ones are facilities, people, taxes, borrowing, and owner's living. That last one seems obvious, but it can be taken for granted. Most people underestimate their living expenses, especially for things like meals, entertainment, and vacations. They will do their planning and only include major expenses. The little costs add up, though, and create problems in your budget.

    You can estimate the aforementioned list using a two to three-year cash flow projection. Use a spreadsheet (I told you I liked spreadsheets) to calculate your budget, payroll, and tax projections. A well-prepared cash flow projection is a wealth of information. As much as possible, your inputs should be real numbers. Get rent costs, utility costs by month, and quotes for insurance. Do your research. Most CPAs, small business development centers, and the Small Business Administration will have similar spreadsheets/tools to help you in this process. Don't skip this process.

A good cash-flow projection can keep you on pace and prepare you for the changes in your revenue. The monthly costs that you identify help you determine your breakeven point—where your revenue equals your costs/expenses. If profit equals income minus expenses, breakeven means that you made enough to cover expenses, but you earned zero profit.

A good way to ensure that you have profit starts by developing a good pricing model. If you sell products, your price should include overhead, labor, inventory cost (cost of goods sold, COGS), and profit. Overhead includes administration costs, fixed costs of facilities, supplies, and the like. Explaining cost accounting is beyond the scope of this book, but you should have a good idea of most of those costs.

If you sell services, your price will include all the same components except for COGS. When you build profit into your pricing model, you are more likely to earn a profit. That sounds so simple, but many contractors or professionals only include their labor and overhead. Then when they start to grow and want to hire someone, they don't understand why they no longer see a profit. Setting the right price structure is worth spending time in analysis. You don't have to do it alone. Call BKM, and we can help you analyze your pricing and sales models. If you don't call us, call someone!

You must count the costs for your E-Hero journey. It may feel like a delay, but great E-Heroes prepare ahead of time. Okay, you have measured your level of dissatisfaction and calculated the potential risks and rewards. You know that while E-Heros have greater freedom, they also have greater (and more complex) responsibilities. You have counted the costs and decided that the best choice for you is to be an entrepreneur. Congratulations! You are ready for the next step on your E-Hero's journey.

The Choice - Chapter Summary

- If you choose self-employment, you choose to leave the nine-to-five life behind and embrace a schedule determined by responsibilities instead of a clock.
- When you start a business, you might think of yourself as a salesperson, a mechanic, and a CPA, but you are also the CEO, CFO, accounting manager, customer service desk, and every other role that you haven't hired yet
- All occupations involve some amount of risk. Both employees and the self-employed must manage that risk.
- The self-employed choose many employers (customers) over a single employer to create job security.
- E-Hero employees get promoted first and are ambitious for the company's mission! Any employee at any level can choose to be an E-Hero. When you decide to give yourself to the position, you

connect with the company and know that your part plays a role in the company's success.
- Before launching as an entrepreneur, prepare a cash-flow projection estimating sales and expenses, specifically paying attention to facilities, people, taxes, borrowing, and owner's living.
- Know your breakeven point and build a pricing model that works profit into every sale.
- After looking at all the figures and facts, keep your "We can do this!" attitude alive!

CHAPTER 5

THE CALL TO LEAD

Luke Skywalker never thought he might lead a rebel attack on an imperial base, much less the Death Star. When we first meet him, he whines to his uncle about having to work the farm one more year. He makes bad decisions like removing restraints from R2-D2. Later, his weakness shows through a near-fatal fight in a bar full of miscreants. Obi-Wan had to bail him out several times. But then, when things get real, pretending to be a storm trooper, he pushes his team to seek out the princess to rescue her.

As an E-Hero, you must rise to the call to become a leader. To own a business, you take on the mantle whether you like it or not! You must first lead yourself through self-improvement before you can lead those around you—vendors, customers, or employees. You will be the one they look to. You make the decisions.

Years ago, I went to New Orleans during Mardi Gras, where loud music, beaded necklaces, and strange drunk people flood the streets each year to celebrate "Fat Tuesday," the day before Lent. A team from our church went to share the Gospel with local party-goers. I had never been there before, but immediately, at 22 years old, I was selected to lead a group of middle-aged women to walk the streets and pass out flyers (or tracts) that shared the Gospel message. My leadership skills weren't that developed, so when we set out, I made the mistake of taking these ladies down Bourbon Street.

> You must first lead yourself through self-improvement before you can lead those around you.

Bourbon Street happens to be where most of the debauchery and craziness happen. At one point during the trip, there were so many people on the street that we were literally body to body. Swaying back and forth but not moving forward, I felt the consequence of my decision. One of the ladies began to hyperventilate; another told us she had been groped. Finally, the dam of bodies broke free, and we were able to get out of there! From then on, I stayed on the perimeter of the excitement.

The call to lead isn't a point on the journey of an E-Hero. It is, however, important enough to address here in the context of when you made "the choice" to embark. If you don't develop your leadership capabilities early on, you may be forced to repeat parts of your journey over and over. Like I found myself and the ladies I led, you will be stuck in a pattern, going nowhere.

Responsibilities Rather Than Tasks

Entrepreneurs think differently than employees. An entrepreneur sees a job as a set of responsibilities, whereas an employee sees it as just a set of tasks. But just like you can choose to become a business owner, you can choose to take ownership of your responsibilities, no matter where you are. When you choose to be an entrepreneur or entrepreneurial employee, you will take responsibility for your company's success. And spending some time as an E-Hero employee may prepare you to take that "on your own" journey in the future.

As a consumer, I have heard an employee tell me, "That's not my job." Nothing frustrates me more. I once contacted a faculty member at a university with questions about something. She responded by giving me the person's contact information in an email reply. That sounds like an appropriate response, right? Wrong. All she did was pass the buck. She didn't see me as a client or customer. I was an inconvenience.

A more appropriate response would have been for her to take responsibility for what they can to get answers to my questions. At the least, she could have forwarded my email to the person who would be able to answer my question. I would still be in the dark, waiting for a response until the next person decided what to do with my question. A better proactive response might have been to reply to me and copy the person who she thought could help. That would have brought everyone into the conversation.

That next level requires an employee to feel some personal responsibility to answer the question, to provide for the company's success.

As you mature, as you get better at serving, seeing your job as a set of responsibilities rather than tasks becomes natural for the E-Hero.

Answer the Call

So, what can you do to release that entrepreneurial spirit, the E-Hero inside? First, answer the call to be a leader. Show up early, leave late (but not too late, life balance is essential). Help those around you reach their potential. The servant-leader model works best. This way, you lead by your actions and not just your words.

At its core, leadership is influence. How you use that influence is up to you. I have seen many employees and business owners use their influence to bring down productivity in others. They find ambition threatening, so they try to squash it as much as possible.

When my kids were younger, I had the privilege to coach little league baseball. For six years, I did my best to teach kids how to throw, catch, and hit a baseball. For two of those years, my assistant coach was a man named Josh Fee. He was a youth pastor at a small Baptist church where we lived. Before taking that position, he had been a teacher and a head coach for a high school varsity baseball team. (That's the manager for those baseball fans reading). Before that, he had played baseball at a Division I college on scholarship.

It wasn't the first time I had an assistant coach who was way more qualified than me. The first year I coached, my assistant coach, also named Josh, was a teacher and softball coach at the high school. Both men made me better at coaching. Josh Fee especially gave me instructions about running practice and drills for pitchers and catchers. He was quiet as an assistant coach, encouraging me as I stumbled through practices and games. Josh showed me what leadership looked like.

In my final year of coaching baseball, our roles switched. Josh became the manager, and I was the assistant coach. As teammates, it was an easy transition. The titles meant less than our purpose; to teach young men how to play baseball.

Be a leader that encourages others to be the best version of themselves. Leaders recognize potential in others and develop that potential. Make that your superpower! Whether you get any recognition for helping others to be successful or not doesn't take away the inner reward of knowing you had a part to play.

> Be a leader that encourages others to be the best version of themselves.

Innovate In Your Area

Next, innovate in your area of responsibility. For employees, what are you responsible for? Is there a better way to achieve what is required? Sometimes companies have systems of doing things dictated by the corporate managers. I'm not saying to buck the system, but working within that system, what minor adjustments can you make to improve efficiency and performance? Get the necessary approvals if you have to, but be proactive.

Let innovation come from any source. You may learn from books or podcasts, or an employee may suggest a better way. Don't feel threatened by great ideas coming from your team. Encourage those you work with—employees, customers, or vendors—to speak up if they see potential for improvement. My firm sends out a short survey to every client after completing a project. These surveys ask for customer input into the process. In addition, we encourage our staff during weekly meetings to share their thoughts on what works and what doesn't. From intern to tax manager, we listen to all ideas.

There is a story about a woman who cooks a ham every year for Thanksgiving. As she prepared the ham for the oven, her husband noticed that she had cut both ends off the ham before placing it in the pan. Curious, he asked, "Why did you cut the ends off the ham?"

She replied, "I don't know; that's just how my mother prepared ham."

Now curious as well, she called her mother to ask why she cut the ends off the ham. Her mother replied, "I just prepare ham the way my mother did."

Since her grandmother was still alive, the woman called her to ask how she prepared her ham for Thanksgiving. "Well, dear," Grandma replied, "I cut the ends off my ham because I didn't have a pan large enough to fit the ham from the market."

The moral of the story is that sometimes you have to question the status quo. You can innovate by asking good questions and making small changes that can have a huge impact on your company's effectiveness and efficiency.

Study For Improvement

Leaders continue to improve their performance, knowledge, and understanding of their responsibilities. When you commit to continuous self-improvement, people will notice. Those who believe that studying ends when you graduate from high school or college will be left behind. You have heard the saying, "Life is a journey." Education is part of that journey. I will speak more on this in later chapters, but for now, you should know that your education did not make you an expert at your job.

After graduating from college with my accounting degree, I couldn't do my own taxes. I received an "A" in my tax courses, but it didn't make me a tax preparer or tax accountant. It did prepare me to learn my job. But, as I learned, I realized I needed more than experience to truly help my clients. I needed others' experience.

Continuing education and reading tax and business books gave me the value of the authors' experiences without the pain of their failures. My clients would often ask about certain tax strategies or were in situations where they needed a tax strategy for which I didn't have the answer. Instead of ignoring that need, I studied it. Reading articles and books on the subject reinforced my understanding and allowed me to serve my clients better. As an E-Hero, become the expert your customers or clients need!

Leaders Are Readers

I have talked to hundreds of CEOs of large and small businesses and listened to thousands of podcasts from multi-millionaire—some billionaire—business owners. They have at least one thing in common: they are avid readers. They consume knowledge like they consume air or food.

One of the business owners I recently talked to reads, or listens to, about twenty-five books per year. I never read much in high school, mainly because the books I was forced to read were of no real interest to me. I liked fiction but could never stay focused and finish those books. The books that captured my attention were usually biographies.

I realized later in life that business books were the biographies of one or more businesses with explanations as to why they succeeded or failed.

Listening to a book on iTunes, Scribd, or Audible while I work out or travel is one of my joys in life. I urge you to learn from the successes and failures of those who have gone before you. Their experiences are captured in books. If you choose not to be a reader, you will be left behind. Your job, company, and relationships will improve when you take the lessons of these resources and apply them.

Applying What You Learn

Business owners sometimes make the mistake of broadcasting to their employees a new "focus and strategy" of the company from every new book they read. This gives your employees and customers whiplash. Instead, take small segments out of these books and take time to think about how to assimilate them into your current strategy, focus, or vision.

Your vision shouldn't change dramatically because of a book you read this week. It can, however, be improved, dialed in, and aligned more clearly. One company CEO read Patrick Lencioni's *The Five Dysfunctions of a Team: A Leadership Fable* and asked all his executive staff to read it. Then, he talked about it for weeks and criticized them for not applying the lessons from the book. It was a disaster. What's worse is that the executive staff now see the text in light of their CEO's imposition and can't stand it.

In contrast, another CEO I know read the same book and then discussed its value with his executive team. In his monthly coaching sessions with the executive team, they were assigned one or two chapters to read before the meeting. As the executive team read the book with their CEO, they agreed on its value and implemented it at all levels of their organization. Then they went through the book's principles with their direct reports in their monthly coaching meetings, down to the lowest levels. Once everyone had gone through it, they made it part of their onboarding process with new hires. The lessons in the book are now part of their culture.

The best way to integrate new knowledge and understanding into your organization is to introduce it slowly, in meaningful ways that allow people the opportunity to consider its merits, weigh in on the discussion, and buy in to the ideas. Your staff will appreciate it; the authors of those books will appreciate it as well.

Receive Coaching

What else do leaders do? They receive coaching. As a business owner, you could hire a business coach. Our firm offers business and real estate investor coaching. Like the voice on your GPS, a coach guides you through traffic to get to your destination.

As an entrepreneurial employee, if your company offers it from your managers, take advantage of this. Even if they aren't great at coaching or criticize you, accept it through the lens of continuous improvement. Take the good, throw out the crap!

Good coaching is very positive. What makes a great coach is asking probing questions that activate your natural learning and creativity. But even if you don't have a great coach, you can be a great team member. The entrepreneur spirit is teachable. If you are paying attention, you can learn as much from watching what not to do as you can from being instructed in best practices.

Once, during my martial arts class, as I demonstrated my form, one of the instructors (whom I didn't care for) gave me some pointers on a difficult part of the form. At the midpoint of the form, some eighty-two moves, I do three round kicks in three different directions without putting my leg down and keeping my knee pointed at my target. At first, when I received her advice, irritated, I mumbled under my breath. Then, I had a moment of clarity. I followed her advice, and it helped.

If I had not had a teachable spirit, I would have continued to have more difficulty in my form. Later, I thanked her for her comments and opened the door for her to make any more comments if she saw something else. She is now one of my favorite instructors. The entrepreneurial spirit allows others to speak into your life.

Serve Like You Own The Place

Finally, what else can you, as a leader, do to release the entrepreneurial spirit? Serve the clients or customers. I was going to say treat them like family, but some families are complicated. Plus, we tend to give our family discounts, so I'm not talking about that or undervaluing your work. Instead, care about customers and their needs. It seems simple, but I have gone through several employees who have not had the same care and concern for my clients as I do, and it showed.

They complain about them, talk negatively about them, or get joy in charging extra fees or selling them things they don't need. An E-Hero can't afford to do that. Why? Because your name is associated with your service. You might squeeze a few more dollars out of a customer, but they won't come back. And then, they will tell fifteen different people how bad their experience was. Now, it's even worse. If they write a bad review, it's forever posted online for the world to see.

As an employer, take notice if you see your clients taken care of by your staff with great care and concern. Rewards those who sincerely care about your clients.

As an E-Hero employee, you are an ambassador of the company you work for. That means that you represent them in how you speak and how you serve. The way you serve connects people to who you are—to your character. Show them the best of yourself by serving them as you would want to be served.

Leadership takes personal awareness, a commitment to continual improvement, having the right attitude, and valuing people. Valuing people is upward, downward, and outward. That is, upward towards your supervisors, downward towards your direct reports, and outward toward clients, customers, or anyone your organization serves.

Whether you are an employee, self-employed, or business owner, you can still be an E-Hero leader. If you are not a leader, you can never be a good employee, self-employed person, or business owner. Leadership abilities distinguish excellence from mediocrity.

Chapter Summary — The Call to Lead

- Becoming an E-Hero is answering a call to lead others. What kind of leader you will be is up to you.
- An E-Hero sees a job as a set of responsibilities; employees see it as just a set of tasks.
- Determine to look for and cultivate potential in others. Be a leader who encourages others to be the best version of themselves.
- Effective leaders look at problems from new angles, question the status quo, keep a fresh perspective, and innovate. This keeps you on the cutting edge.
- Never stop improving. Leaders are learners. Leaders are readers. Your job, company, and relationships will improve when you take the lessons from books, articles, podcasts, blogs, mentors, and coaches and apply them.
- Lead by serving. Serve people—your customers, vendors, and employees—the way you want to be served. If you keep the right attitude and demonstrate value for people, your influence—leadership—will grow.

CHAPTER 6

THE GOAL

Luke sat in Obi-Wan's cave cleaning out R2D2 when he stumbled on a piece of a secret message by Princess Leia. As he worked, Obi-Wan handed him a light saber—one that had belonged to Luke's father. The moment was thick with destiny.

Suddenly, Leia's full message played, and she pleaded for Obi-Wan's help to fight the Empire. Something stirred deep inside Luke, and the tension between the life he knew and the life he desired was palpable.

Luke was moved by his dissatisfaction. He wanted to do something bigger and more meaningful than work his uncle's farm, and saving Princess Lea was the initial goal of his hero's journey. But do you think Obi-Wan believed saving the princess was the goal or just one of the obstacles they would face along the way? From prequels, we later learn that Obi placed himself on that planet to watch over Luke and protect him from the Emperor. So, his goals for Luke must have been in the making for decades.

Like Luke, your E-Hero goals might not be as apparent as you think. Sometimes it takes a while to discover your vision.

Obi-Wan knew that if the Republic were to survive, it would need Luke Skywalker to become a Jedi. Obi-Wan saw the goal much broader than Luke. He wasn't just there to save the princess; he was there to save the Republic!

Your Vision

In college, I was required to read *The Goal* by Eliyahu M. Goldratt. I liked it very much. The book introduced the world to the *theory of constraints.* It was an operations manual, written as a novel, about how any process is only as fast as its slowest component. Another premise is that the goal of any company is to make money. That makes sense, right? You pay your bills with cash, so it makes sense that your goal is to make money. But alas, no. The common purpose of maximizing shareholder value or "making money" is hollow and self-serving.

While profits are necessary to stay in business, this can't be the company's purpose. No business can grow beyond its owner with a purpose statement like that. When many small businesses start, they are a means to provide for the owner's family. That is as good a purpose as any. However, as you grow, the scope of your business purpose must be broader to inspire your employees.

There are now businesses whose sole purpose is to provide jobs for a people group or provide shoes to children in the developing world. Providing for others is a great mission or purpose statement. I use these words interchangeably.

There are many books on this topic where the author usually defines the terms: mission, vision, and purpose. I have read many, and definitions sometimes differ, but the underlying theme is similar. The mission statement is the reason your business exists, its purpose. Your vision includes the mission statement and defines who you are, your core values, where you are going, and your big hairy audacious goals (BHAGs). Let's take a few paragraphs to unpack that last line.

Your Values

Take a minute to sit back and evaluate who you are. What is most important to you? What makes you, you? You chose to be an entrepreneur. Why? What was the motivation behind that? Now that you made that choice, what kind of entrepreneur will you be?

Meditate on your values, then finish this statement:

I would never work in a place that didn't _____.

What words or phrases did you choose? Some examples are innovate, value family, have fun, commit to the customers and me. When you get about twenty answers to that question, find four to seven that are the most important to you. Then ask yourself why they are important to you.

Remember, this new business is a *reflection of you*. Some businesses have one-word value lists. I prefer value phrases. Or, if you want that one word, have a sentence or phrase with it that defines the word for your company. For example, the word might be *commitment* and then an explanatory phrase, such as, "We are committed to each other and our customers." This process isn't and shouldn't be quick. It should take at least a few hours and deserves time to let the thoughts develop, rest, and review before printing and posting them as permanent.

Sometimes it is best to have someone else, like a business coach, help walk you through the process. You should include some of your staff in the process, especially if you already have a business and an executive team.

Your Purpose

Now that you have identified your core values and your business core values, you need to take the next step to define the purpose for your business. Why does your business exist? Keep in mind the core values you just identified. Your purpose can't contradict your values.

I like to define this purpose by starting with what you do, or are proposing to do, as a new business and then asking why? And then ask why again. After about the fourth "why," you should have gotten to the root purpose.

You might start with, "We make barbecue sandwiches, brisket, sausage, and sides." Then ask why? "Because we know how to make those better than anyone in town, and they sell better than hamburgers." Then ask why again? "Because our family gave us the recipe, we have perfected it, and we want our customers to share in the joy of good pulled pork and brisket." Why? "Because we are filled with joy when we see our customers smile after taking their first bite."

After examining these responses, your purpose statement might be: "To share our family recipes with our customers and see the joy in their eyes and on their faces after taking that first bite of the best pulled pork and brisket in the world!" That seems a simple exercise, but it usually takes a while to work through and a couple more times asking why.

A good facilitator won't let you stop until you have uncovered your true purpose. You can see that this process is truly self-reflecting. It has to be. When you face external and internal obstacles in the future, your core values and purpose will be tested. Those tests happen along the way to see your goals become a reality.

Meaning and Purpose

There is a real call for meaning and purpose beyond just making money in today's business culture, especially among young people. They want to know that what they are doing isn't just for creating wealth for the shareholders. Meaning is what you derive from past efforts, while purpose is the reason to expend any present or future effort. For many people, their job is a way to fund their hobbies. Sometimes these hobbies are noble, like volunteering in their community or with organizations that serve developing countries.

Sometimes these hobbies are just sad, like playing video games or paintball. I'm not dissing on paintball. I love paintball. But I don't think paintball can be the "purpose" behind work. You may not like video games, but don't dismiss them as childish. They are an enjoyable escape for some, especially on rainy days. However, they also cannot be your purpose (unless you are a professional gamer or game tester like my kids have aspired to off and on in their youth).

You're an E-Hero. That means you must help your team members find meaning and purpose in their work. I once believed my job encompassed being the best tax accountant, financial advisor, and real estate investor I could be. Now, I know that my purpose is leading and developing people to become their best selves. I do this at my firm, at my church, and with my family and friends. My purpose permeates every part of my life.

The type of work you do is irrelevant when you have a purpose. Just like the example of sharing great barbecue with customers to see their joy, the food of choice doesn't matter. While Walt Disney was alive, his purpose was simply to make children and their parents happy—to experience "the happiest place on earth." The Disney corporation may now exist to create socialist bots who blindly follow government leadership, but that is another book.

> The type of work you do is irrelevant when you have a purpose.

Clarity of Vision

When you are a small operation, connecting with your team is easy. Your values flow out of you because they *are* you. Your purpose, though it may not be stated, is evident in how you interact with your customers. Every time you smile when they smile, your employees see what makes you tick. When you grow larger and are not around the new employees much, how do you relay that purpose? In his book, *The Four Obsessions of an Extraordinary Executive*, Patrick Lencioni answers that question:

1. Teamwork
2. Clarity

3. Communication about clarity
4. Reinforcing clarity

So basically, teamwork and clarity. It is not enough to list your values in the employee handbook and never talk about them again. It is not enough to have your mission statement posted on the wall and never mention it again. It is not enough to list your goals in your journal and never talk about them to your staff or team members. Gain clarity, obsess over them and communicate them well. Then communicate them again. And again. Every team member should know your mission, values, goals, and objectives.

In my firm, we struggled for years with high turnover. I would train someone, and then they would find a job somewhere else. It was frustrating. I had a dream to be a more prominent firm regionally; at the time, my vision only expanded throughout Texas. But no one knew my plans. No one understood our purpose or had a real grasp of the firm's values. All decision-making, even the smallest of decisions, fell on me.

It was tough. We expanded into the North Austin market, and I thought that would help our staff understand the vision. It only confused them. Some staff and clients wondered if I just did that to move there and shut the West Texas firm down. When I heard these things, I was in disbelief.

I decided to start doing a semiannual firm meeting mainly because team members in North Austin had never met the West Texas team in person. It was a two-day gathering to discuss best practices, some operations issues, and some educational items. I decided that I would open the meetings with our firm's vision.

I finally wrote it down. We talked about our values, where we were now, and where we wanted to be. I couldn't tell what happened in that meeting until much later. My team finally understood what was important to me and where we were going. We still have turnover, but not nearly as much, and I can mark that meeting as the turning point.

Big Hairy Audacious Goals (BHAGs)

Let's talk about setting goals, the target that every company should have. Jim Collins defined BHAGs in his book *Good to Great: Why Some Companies Make The Leap … And Others Don't,* and also in the updated book he co-authored with William Lazier, *Beyond Entrepreneurship 2.0: Turning Your Business Into An Enduring Great Company.* Both of these make my "You Should Read" list found in the appendix.

BHAGs must be attainable but not easy. Set your Big Hairy Audacious Goals at ten, fifteen, to twenty years out. It's a target on the horizon. It must be something that will draw people in and inspire them, like President Kennedy declaring that we would put an American on the moon by the end of the decade. Or like my firm declaring we would be an entirely virtual firm with employees working remotely across the nation. Then once that was a reality, "We will make the current CPA firm irrelevant, be nationally known, and serve clients in all 50 states in seven years!"

These BHAGs aren't necessarily financially driven—although increased profitability is a natural result. Instead, you should find a BHAG that will stir excitement in you and your staff. It's hard to get employees excited and pumped up to make money for the owners. But challenge them to become better and do better, and they will rise to the challenge.

Charles Schwab, the first person to receive a salary over one million dollars, once challenged the production floor of US Steel to do better by simply writing a number in chalk on the floor. That number represented how many batches the day shift produced that day. In the morning, the day shift found their number wiped off the floor and replaced by a bigger number by the night shift.

People want to be challenged. Sometimes competition creates the best challenge. That's why one of our BHAGs states that we will make the traditional CPA firm irrelevant! With that statement, we declared that we are different, and through innovation and technology, we would set the course for the industry and not follow it.

Your Strategy

With your BHAGs written down and now looking for the next step towards that goal, you can think about strategy. Strategy is the HOW. How will you get closer to achieving your BHAG? Coming up with strategies takes some time and the effort of forethought.

You must ensure that your chosen strategies align with your values and create your desired results. Sometimes people with good intentions create strategies that produce the opposite of what they want. Those unintended results should send you back to the whiteboard to find new strategies. That isn't a failure; it's learning.

The strategies you employ can change, especially if they don't work, but they shouldn't change much. You can wear your people out if you float from strategy to strategy without giving the current one time to succeed or fail. The larger the organization, the longer it takes for strategies to work. That's what people mean when they say that smaller companies are lean and agile. Companies don't dance or work out; they move into and out of markets, strategies, locations, etc.

What makes larger companies slower is convincing their people that the next strategy will work if applied. The more people you have to convince, the longer it takes to adjust your course. For our firm, we chose four strategic anchors to reach our BHAGs. First, we provide superior professional tax and accounting services in a virtual environment. Second, we hire the best people and release them to do excellent work. Third, we target our niche of anything to do with real estate; real estate investors, realtors, mortgage brokers, and construction companies. As a real estate investor myself, we are ideally positioned to help others in the industry.

Finally, we make our services and presence known on the world wide web through targeted marketing campaigns, subscription packages, and useful content for niche groups. That's the current BKM strategy, and we'll continue to assess and adjust as needed to reach our goals. Next, let's discuss tactics.

Your Tactics

Tactics are the activities performed to execute the strategy. These can change more often than strategies, focusing on people, systems, and processes. Your software might change, but until you meet your goal, the strategy won't change. Your people might come and go or be moved from seat to seat, but the strategy won't change until you meet your goal. Your processes might change, but the goals and strategies are still your focus.

For example, we have had a change in tax software on multiple occasions. This did not affect the firm's clients. We made the change because we believed the features of the tax software would enhance the execution of the strategy, not change it.

When you grow, sometimes it is necessary to move people into different seats. I had a gifted tax preparer move into the accounting department because I wanted my best teammate on our strategy's greatest opportunity. People changed seats in the firm, but the vision, mission, and values did not change.

Setting your tactics depends on your organization's strengths, weaknesses, opportunities, and threats. Before you decide on the tactics to meet those strategies, do a strategic S.W.O.T. analysis by asking the following questions:

1. How can we match our **strengths** with the **opportunities** we see?
2. How can we use our **strengths** to overcome the known **threats**?
3. What do we do to ensure that our **weaknesses** won't sabotage our opportunities?
4. What action do we need to take to avoid our **weaknesses** combining with the known **threats**?

Answering these questions gives you a long list of possible tactics to follow. Now, choose the two or three activities within each strategic focus that will have the greatest impact for the company. Once activities are selected, you must decide who will be responsible for each activity and when those activities should be completed.

You know who you are—your values. You know your mission—your reason for being. You know where you are going—your *big hairy audacious goals,* how you are going to get there, and the strategies and tactics that will get the job done. With thoughtful consideration of these elements, you are on course.

Once committed to your course, another important element of reaching your goals is relying on the potential and development of your people. Let's turn our attention now to unleashing that potential!

The Goal - Chapter Summary

- Vision includes your mission statement and defines who you are, your core values, and where you are going, your big hairy audacious goals (BHAGs).
- To identify your company's values, finish this statement: I would never work in a place that didn't (or wasn't) _____. What words or phrases did you choose?
- To define your mission, start with what you do, or propose to do as a new business, and then ask why? Then ask why again. After about the fourth (or fifth) "why," you should get to the root purpose.
- Meaning is what you derive from past efforts, while purpose is the reason to expend any present or future effort.

- How do you relay your purpose when you grow and are no longer around new employees? By focusing on teamwork, clarity of purpose, communicating clarity, and reinforcing clarity.
- Every company should have short-term and long-term goals (BHAGs), some financial, others inspirational.
- Strategy is HOW you will get closer to achieving your BHAG? Coming up with strategies takes some time and the effort of forethought. You must ensure that your chosen strategies align with your values and create your desired results.
- Tactics are the activities performed to execute the strategy. These can change more often than the strategies and focus on people, systems, and processes.

CHAPTER 7

THE POTENTIAL UNLEASHED

"We have found my enemy ... and he is us!" Walt Kelly.

In fiction novels, the main characters often are part of two or more different stories or arcs. Sometimes called the "B-Story," the sideline plot happens at the same time the main arc occurs. In the *Matrix*, the B-Story revolves around how Trinity falls in love with Neo, which could only mean that he is "the one." Ironically, he is the one for her and also the prophetic "one."

For E-Heroes, the main story arc centers on your vision and the life of your business. The secondary story, and probably just as important, focuses on the people around you. Those people who come along as advisors, employees, partners, and vendors. Your role as the E-hero can impact their life dramatically.

Sometimes we are our own worst enemy. I have been an arrogant, critical son-of-a-bitch for most of my life. I know it's true. Just ask my friends. Yes, even critical, arrogant sons of bitches can have friends ... for a while. So, if you are reading this book and we met in the first 40 or so years of my life, let me take this opportunity to ask for forgiveness. I am deeply sorry for how I treated you.

I can't say that I have fixed every issue in my life. All I can say is that I have become very aware of my learned behavior and am trying to unlearn it. You see, I come from a very critical family. Even writing that makes me feel bad. The irony of that statement is that I am critical of my critical family. Dang, that sucks. But enough about me, let's save something for my therapist.

Culture of Trust

Let's move forward into how you and I can replace this kind of behavior with a culture of trust and encouragement. There are several books about building trust within your organization. Be sure to check out my "You Should Read" list in the appendix for some of my favorite books on trust and team building. You can't do one without the other.

Trust remains the foundation of building good teams. If you don't trust that the other members of your team are looking out for your best interest, you won't work for their best interest. I would rather have a teammate I can trust over someone with more talent. So how do you build trust? Stephen Covey describes thirteen behaviors of high trust leadership. All center around a few key attributes:

1. Responsibility—keeping commitments, confronting reality, delivering results, showing loyalty
2. Accountability—getting better, clarifying expectations, stewardship

3. Awareness and Respect—listening first, extending trust, demonstrating respect
4. Vulnerability and Improvement—getting better, righting wrongs, creating transparency, talking straight
5. Integrity and honesty—talking straight, creating transparency, righting wrongs, showing loyalty

These behaviors will build a foundation of trust amongst your team. Especially number four, being vulnerable and committed to self-improvement. You might think that being vulnerable will put others off or diminish your authority. It doesn't. In fact, it draws people into your life. They almost feel obligated to share their life when you open up and share yours.

There are also a ton of books on leadership. John C. Maxwell has built a career on training and developing leaders. To be an effective leader, you have to be teachable, humble, and on a path of continuous improvement. You can never stop learning.

The best way is to activate the natural learning process that every person is born with. When you learned to walk, no one gave you written or verbal instructions on how to walk. Instead, you became aware of your body and what it could do. Then you tried and failed an innumerable number of times until you began to be a walker.

In the book, *The Inner Game of Tennis: The Classic Guide To The Mental Side Of Peak Performance* (yes, this makes my list), W. Timothy Gallwey discusses this process. In it, Gallwey describes the *instruction method* of coaching versus *the active learning method* of coaching.

Active Learning

For active learning to occur, we have to stop listening to the inner voices in our heads (Self 1) and allow our true self (Self 2) to come through. Before I read the book, I had an experience with my middle son, Ian, on the mountain in Ruidoso, New Mexico trying to teach him how to ski. He was seven or eight at the time.

I tried to give him instructions on how to slow down, stop, speed up, and turn by *telling* him how to do it. It was very frustrating. Especially since this kid, unlike other kids his age, was and still is a highly-gifted athlete. He'd had a very high level of hand-eye coordination before he could walk.

He amazed people at age five with his skill in playing baseball, fielding ground balls, batting, throwing, and running the bases. No one ever taught Ian how to ride a bicycle. I was at work, and one of the neighbor kids told him to ride his bike without the training wheels. So he did. This made what I saw on the mountain completely puzzling to me.

At one point on the lift, he said, "Dad, I'm sorry I'm not doing well. Please don't be mad at me." Hearing that broke my heart.

I said to him, "Son, I'm not upset with you. I'm upset with myself. I'm not doing a good job teaching and am upset that you aren't having much fun."

By the way, I also accidentally ran my ski into his shin after he had fallen when I tried to get to him quickly to "help." That added to my disgust with myself (my Self 1 criticizing me on how I was doing). Then, as I watched him attempt to ski, it hit me. He was thinking about everything I told him instead of trying to ski.

In a moment of divine brilliance, I told him to stop looking at his skis and to look where he was going. I said, "Don't worry about all the stuff I told you. Just ski. Your body knows what to do." And then, just like that, he was the athletic prodigy once more. He was shifting and moving fast, then slowing down, as if he had been skiing for years. It was like someone turned a switch, and the light came on.

Once he was aware of his body and not consumed with all the instructions, natural active learning was restored. I have told that story a hundred times without understanding what actually happened until after I read Gallwey's book.

You can engage your team in active learning by asking probing questions instead of instructing them like I instructed Ian. People are creative and resourceful. Often you can get great results by not saying anything at all. Just tell them what you need and see how they respond.

Coaching Culture

Create a coaching culture to help you cultivate active learning within yourself and those around you. Coaching eliminates criticism and replaces it with curiosity. Criticism kills relationships. There is no place for criticism in leadership or business. In his book *Coaching for Performance: The Principles and Practice of Coaching and Leadership,* Sir John Whitmore says that performance equals potential minus distractions.

To eliminate distractions and fully maximize performance (yours or your

> Criticism kills relationships. There is no place for criticism in leadership or business.

employees), you must engage awareness and responsibility. I'm not going to rewrite Whitmore's book here, but highlight that the way to unleash your potential is to eliminate criticism—self-criticism and criticism of others.

You are not responsible for how other people feel; you are not responsible for their emotions. You are responsible for how you respond to information, input, and stimulus from the world around you. Most people react. That's impulsive, thoughtless, and has negative consequences. Do your best to respond. That's calm, thoughtful, and careful. From here, you use words without judgment and criticism.

For example, I had a staff member tell a client incorrect information, and the client became livid. So much so that he left our firm. The old me would have asked the staff member, "Why the hell did you say that?" Anytime you use the word "Why," you are accusing and judging them for their behavior. A better question would be, "What information led you to that conclusion?" or "What was the issue the client needed to be addressed?"

These questions ask for facts, not feelings or analysis. These open-ended questions help you to gain understanding. And without judgments. Had I approached with an accusatory tone, the staff member would not learn from the experience—other than to fear retribution for mistakes. Instead, they would become even more dependent on others to think for them. Criticism discourages people from being proactive or owning their decisions. They are more prone to "cover your ass" behavior and protect themselves by doing only and exactly as they are told.

A coaching culture eliminates criticism and encourages awareness and responsibility. You can help unleash your team's potential. It takes patience on your part and learning how to ask great questions.

Self-Awareness

You don't have to wait for others to make mistakes to begin this type of interaction. You can have it within yourself on a regular basis. You can change your inner self-talk from critical to curious. Ask yourself probing questions, and you will increase your self-awareness and natural learning. It has helped me. I can tell a huge difference in how my team interacts with me and each other.

It must start with you as the hero entrepreneur. Become aware of how you respond to and interact with people. Identify what makes you angry, sad, or overwhelmed. And then dig deeper as to what creates those triggers. If you need to go to counseling to get there, please do. I have and will continue to use a counselor/therapist.

Not all counselors are alike. I prefer ones who act more like life coaches than academics. Those who ask good probing questions without judgment or condemnation are the best. Someone close to me went to a counselor who talked most of the session, and then after my friend did get to speak, the counselor just labeled her and spoke *at* her. I'm not sure if she will ever go to another therapist.

In one of my counseling sessions, I mentioned that I get bored after I find some success. Then I tried to move on and talk about other things. He stopped me and said we needed to dive a bit deeper there. He asked, "What do you think is the reason you get bored?" It was the end of our session, so I had a while to think about that question.

My answer was, "I believe I have more potential than I am currently experiencing." That question led to a host of other questions that I am still working through. This exercise is life-changing. It is the continuous improvement of self.

Developing People

Unleashing your potential is one thing; helping others around you unleash their potential is the most rewarding exercise I have undertaken. To see people develop into their best selves and find success and fulfillment makes work fun.

You're an E-Hero. You need to see the purpose and meaning in your work. It isn't just about making money but making the world, your world, a better place to live. That includes helping your staff become leaders, acquire certifications, and meet their professional goals.

When my team members and I meet for our monthly coaching sessions, we discuss their one-page plan. It has where they are now, where they want to be, and how they are going to get there. We discuss those three parts in various areas of their professional life.

As their coach and boss, my role is to help them map out their professional plans. It may surprise you, but I don't care if those plans include our firm. I certainly want each and every staff person to feel welcome, challenged, productive, and enjoyment with us. But, if they believe that their growth will one day take them away from us, that's okay with me.

I won't stand in the way of any of their dreams or goals. Once I received a call from a CPA firm in Abilene. One of my interns, Chris, had interviewed with them, and they were calling to check references. The representative on the call asked if Chris was competent and capable. I replied, "Of course, he's one of the best interns we've had!"

She said, "Well, we weren't that impressed with his appearance, so we thought we would call you and ask."

"Sure, I think you would be very happy with his work," I said.

"Well," she continued, "we have hired several people from your firm and were very happy with their abilities and knowledge. We just wanted to check on Chris."

Apparently, my interns were the farm team for that CPA firm! I should have asked for some compensation for training their staff! It honestly doesn't bother me to hear that someone I trained excels wherever they go. I'm thankful for the time I have with them and take pride in their success.

Fulfillment in Work

There's an old joke I love about farmers. It says, "All farmers go to heaven. Why? Because it wouldn't be right to live your whole life as a farmer and then go to hell too!" Think about all the people you come in contact with during the day. Some who have been in their "jobs" for years and hate it. I just can't imagine living like that.

There is so much joy and fulfillment in this life if you look at it through the entrepreneur's eyes. Note I didn't say happiness—being happy is a moment-to-moment state. Joy is something that comes from within and only from being fulfilled.

My oldest son, Conner, and I were talking about work recently. He just started working for someone other than dad. He has discovered the satisfaction of a hard day's work from this job. Knowing that you have accomplished something and have given it your best is truly satisfying. The joy in work is putting all of that together, doing something fulfilling, and giving it your best.

To be fulfilled in their work, your employees must have three things happening simultaneously: they must actively learn, enjoy their coworkers and work environment, and be productive in their tasks and activities.

As the employer, you can help your employees find fulfillment in what they do. You can't make them give their best. But if they are fulfilled in their work, they will willingly offer their best. If they can't find fulfillment with you, help them find it somewhere else.

You may not be able to find them a new job, but you can have conversations that lead them to discover what might be fulfilling. Some jobs are just temporary, like for high school and college students. If you are in one of these jobs, use it as a learning experience.

I can tell you what I learned at every job since I started working at fourteen years old. Even from the jobs I hated,

> To be fulfilled in their work, your employees must have three things happening simultaneously: they must actively learn, enjoy their coworkers and work environment, and be productive in their tasks and activities.

with bosses I couldn't stand, I learned *something*. You can unleash your potential and your employees' potential. It really is unlimited.

With that goal in mind, you and the people around you can be released to their full potential. You are on your way to the "better life!" Speaking of the better life, next, let's look at the business life curve and make sure we stay fully engaged for the long haul.

The Potential Unleashed - Chapter Summary

- Trust remains the foundation of building good teams. If you don't trust that the team members are looking out for your best interest, you won't work for their best interest.
- These five things build a foundation of trust amongst your team: responsibility, accountability, awareness and respect, vulnerability and improvement, integrity and honesty.
- You engage your team in active learning when you ask probing questions.
- Create a coaching culture to help you cultivate active learning within yourself and those around you. Coaching eliminates criticism and replaces it with curiosity. Criticism kills relationships.
- To eliminate distractions and fully maximize performance, you must engage awareness and responsibility.
- You can change your inner self-talk from critical to curious. Ask yourself probing questions and

increase your self-awareness and your natural learning.
- Help your staff become leaders, acquire certifications, and meet their professional goals.
- To be fulfilled in their work, your employees must have three things happening simultaneously: they must actively learn, enjoy their coworkers and work environment, and be productive in their tasks and activities.

CHAPTER 8

THE BUSINESS LIFE CURVE

Luke Skywalker had an arduous road ahead of him. It seemed to get harder and harder as he went along. The life of an action hero rarely sees moments of calm. The author does that on purpose. Whether the hero climbs an actual mountain or the path makes a more metaphorical incline, the purpose and theme of the story lie in the struggle.

Like many authors do before they write, I want to add this chapter as a potential storyboard for you—the E-Hero. It contains a description of each phase an entrepreneur takes moving towards their goal. This chapter on *the business life curve* takes a step back and looks at the journey from the outside. You may be a seasoned business owner or just starting out. Since I don't know that, we will look at your business hypothetically and follow the typical growth and decline stages.

When I was in college, I had every minute of every day scheduled. I carried a planner everywhere I went to make sure I didn't miss something. I planned time to eat, study, play with my kids, and sleep. It was a brutal schedule, especially the last year. I kept telling myself, "I can do anything for a season." I graduated with my Bachelor of Business Administration from Angelo State University on May 12, 2000. I remember that day as if it were yesterday. I also remember how strange it felt not to have to study anymore.

Because my day planner had ruled my life, I was at a loss about what to do with myself after work or after nine pm. That season of my life had been attending college. When it was over, I faced new challenges, new periods of growth, and then new periods of leveling out into what most people call normal life.

But those times are short for me. Whenever things begin to stabilize, I look for new challenges. If you were to draw a graph of my life, it would look very similar to the *business life curve*. A slow and gradual curve moving to a peak, then a decline in activity, then another period of quiet and gradual movement towards another peak. Unfortunately, most businesses don't reach for new peaks. After they hit a certain level, they begin their period of decline.

Many small business owners are not entrepreneurs. As a CPA, I have encountered small business owners, many of whom have some level of success yet have no desire to grow. I am sure that when they began in business, they had some entrepreneurial spirit in them; however, at some point, the candle of that flame was extinguished.

> Many small business owners are not entrepreneurs.

Some business academics and consultants call the business life curve the business life cycle. I contend that it isn't a cycle because you never return to the initial launch. Many ill-prepared businesses will ultimately capitulate to a buyout, the owner will retire, or the company will die; it will have an end. That is why I prefer the term *business life curve*.

Initial Launch

Business life begins with the *initial launch*. This period has a lot of stress, trauma, and hair-thin margins. Most businesses die during this phase if not appropriately managed or capitalized. Here, you are marketing like crazy with friends, family, and anyone who will listen.

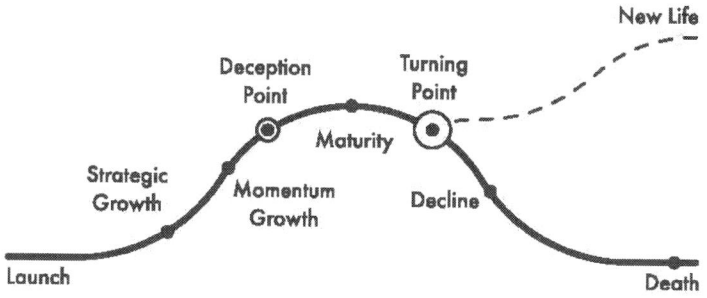

What does it take to launch? You need some structure in place: a business, a name, banking set up, capital to buy supplies and inventory, and possibly a limited liability entity like a Limited Liability Company (LLC). Please reach out to BKM or your business advisor before you launch. It will save you some time and headaches.

There isn't usually a strategy yet for gaining new customers during the initial launch. Asking your business advisor to help you form a strategy for your launch is wisdom. Notwithstanding, most entrepreneurs are do-it-yourselfers and will go it alone. All advertising that you can afford, you will try.

You have social media platforms available that allow for more marketing opportunities than in the past. The old methods still work, too, radio, yellow pages (now the yellow pages connect to web search engines with links to your website), billboards, and local sponsorships of events and youth sports teams, among other things.

Connecting the old and the new is a good strategy too, but in the *initial launch*, you are looking for all the free advertising you can get. Cash is tight, but the willingness to do whatever it takes to make money is loose. It's important to focus on the one to three strategies that will deliver the most impact. Business owners can spend thousands of dollars on one strategy and receive no economic benefit. At the same time, some of the best free strategies create an enormous financial impact.

Often, new businesses offer a long list of product or service offerings. If a customer wants something not on the list, you will sometimes get it or do it anyway to keep them happy. Here you are living a bit out of fear. You don't want to say no if it means losing business.

When I first started, I wouldn't turn down work from anyone. At some point, I started receiving referrals from other CPAs for work that they didn't want. Usually, it was people who hadn't filed their tax returns in several years. Now, I still accept those clients, but only on my terms. Sometimes those terms dissuade potential clients from being clients, and that's okay.

When you begin your business, take some time to think about some niche industries or markets that you can serve. List about ten markets that you know something about. Then, identify which niche areas you would enjoy working with. Focus all your marketing efforts on one or two niche areas rather than trying to win the world.

Strategic Growth

The next stage is *strategic growth*. At this stage, your business should have a pretty good understanding of its values, mission, and goals, so it can act strategically to build a customer base and revenues. Sometimes the process is informal, instinctive even, but it is necessary to get to the next stage. In the beginning, you are like a shotgun of services. Now, you have learned that trimming down the offerings and focusing on a few things (industries, niches) that you do well is better for you (and your family) and better for customer satisfaction.

> Focus all your marketing efforts on one or two niche areas rather than trying to win the world.

Marketing gets more precise. You know better as to what works and what doesn't. You learn not from questionnaires or focus groups but from your conversations with the customers. You're probably still doing everything yourself, but that's because you can't afford to hire anyone. Also, you may have trust issues and have a hard time letting others come in to help. The "flywheel" moves more consistently, and you begin to see cash flow, maybe even a profit.

In *strategic growth,* you know who your customer is and why they buy from you. So, you put all our efforts and time into those things that bring those customers back. When you find a product or service model that works, you stick with it. This is a good mentality right now, but later, it may, in fact, hurt you when the market changes or technology changes. But for you, today, it works.

Most people think that *strategic growth* will come automatically. It doesn't.

Growth may come from your instincts, but you follow intuition with action. You can also get help for this stage. Hiring a business coach or someone to focus your vision is a great way to see *strategic growth*. One of my friends, the CEO of a successful IT company, said they began to see this after a consultant facilitated a meeting with their executive team. They went from 35 employees to over 150 in just a few short years.

A business coach will guide you through the process of identifying your values and writing down your BHAGs. They will also help you problem-solve when things get tough. A business coach makes a great accountability partner for your company. They will see things you can't see because they are on the outside looking in.

A business coach will focus on people, processes, and systems. We have mentioned these before, but now it's time to develop them.

People refers to your organizational chart. When you built the chart at the beginning, you were responsible for every role. Now, you employ people to manage certain roles and responsibilities for you. Remember, anyone you hire should share your values and fit your culture.

Processes refer to how you do business. Onboarding clients, fulfilling orders, delivering services. Each operation must follow a consistent process. You, the owner, might write these down or deliver them personally to each person you hire. You might decide that you require a policy and procedures manual. You need these things out of your head and recorded somewhere for your company to grow.

Systems are the tools you use to move your products and services to the public. You might use apps on your phone, a point of sale system at your cash register, or some payment system on your website. These systems, whether software or pen and paper, need to be evaluated for their effectiveness and efficiency.

The strategic growth phase opens the door to new possibilities. Before this phase, you didn't know if you would make it. Now you can see the horizon. Your expectations grow for this new venture.

Momentum Growth

From there, if your business has made the right moves, it will press past *strategic growth* into the *momentum growth* stage. Here it seems all too easy to gain customers. Referrals might be high; the business may be well known in its market. The proverbial "flywheel" now spins on its own. There are processes in place, the right people are in the right seats, and it seems like you can do nothing wrong. It is also sometimes called the sustaining stage—warning; there is a deception that everything is going well. Revenues are up, and costs are down; everything looks great on the surface. Truthfully, it may be the beginning of the end.

Growing pains begin to creep into your processes. You finally hired some employees, but some may not have the same values, hurting your client relationships. Those clients are loyal right now, but they may be compelled to find another business to support if things continue like this.

The most significant issues in this stage are:

- capacity,
- quality control,
- responsiveness,
- and competition.

Competition is especially important to pay attention to. If you are a new idea in a market, competitors will come out of the woodwork. Most of the issues you face now are due to growth because you got better at serving your customers in the *strategic growth* phase.

The *momentum growth* stage can last several years. As long as you, as the business owner, have not hit your leadership lid, the business can continue to grow internally. Also, if the market conditions don't change dramatically, the company can continue to grow externally in sales and market share.

Have you ever heard the phrase "wheels-off?" I first heard this phrase in 2001 when I was an auditor for Arthur Andersen. It is derived from the idea of a vehicle moving so fast that all the mechanical parts begin to vibrate and unravel. Imagine this car barreling down the interstate, and pieces of the body begin to drop off; then, as the lug nuts shear through immense pressure, the vehicle hurls its wheels and guts everywhere, coming to a crashing halt.

The vehicle's own propulsion pushed it forward until momentum reduced the amount of effort it needed. The driver then put the pedal to the metal to see how fast it could go before the inevitable "wheels-off" moment. Momentum isn't a bad thing, and you need it to see your BHAGs become a reality. But when you approach that moment, before you accelerate, test your processes, systems, and people to determine if the company can handle it. If it can't, pull back on the throttle and work on those areas.

Maturity Stage

The next stage on *the business life curve* is the *maturity stage*. Here, the current market is saturated. Revenues have peaked, and new business is hard to come by. Capacity becomes a real issue. It was probably an issue in the *momentum growth* phase as well, but no one noticed it since revenues were still going up.

Your business has stagnated in many areas. It has failed to change its methods while keeping in line with its values, mission, and goals. It may also have failed to set new goals once the previous ones have been achieved. In many cases, businesses that reach this stage are no longer concerned with growth, internally or externally.

Change is a necessary part of business. Success has to do with several factors, starting with you—the business owner. Do you want to learn and develop? Are you willing to change your methods? Remember when we said that creating a process on how to serve customers is good in the *strategic growth* stage, but later it could hurt the business. Now is when it begins to hurt the business.

"We have always done it this way!" you say. Yet, the market and technology are leaving your business behind. Your business desperately needs new vision and new goals to reignite passion in you and your key employees.

Maturity should imply a better stage in the life curve. Unfortunately, here, maturity means past its prime ("over the hill"). Not all businesses move into the maturity phase. Like *Aerosmith*, who has top ten hits in over four decades, you can continue to be relevant to your customers.

How do you stay relevant with your customers?

Ask them. Use surveys, phone calls, and whatever else you need to keep connecting with your clients. Follow them on social media. Whatever it takes to ensure that you still provide a service they need in a way they want.

If your business has stagnated, you will either reach for a new challenge and climb a new hill or begin that slow decline … leading to a permanent "We're Closed" sign on your door.

Decline and Death

We have now arrived at the last two stages on the backside of the curve, *decline* and *death*. Blockbuster Video is a prime example of the *maturity stage* seeping into *decline* and *death*.

In its *momentum stage,* Blockbuster could boast of more than eight thousand stores and over $5 billion in revenue. It had the opportunity to buy Netflix in 2000 for just $50 million, but Blockbuster couldn't imagine the evolution of their industry moving away from VHS rentals.

That same year CEO John Antioco was approached by Netflix founder Reed Hastings to partner with Blockbuster.

Antioco said no, and the rest is history. By the time Blockbuster decided to get into streaming video services, it was too late. If Blockbuster had moved into streaming video or mail-out DVDs in 1997, they might still be here today.

Don't be Blockbuster.

Throughout all the stages, there is time for change. A new vision or goal can be set; a rebirth of old products and services or new products and services can be implemented to start the curve over again and reboot the *strategic growth* stage. You are at a crossroads. A choice must be made. If nothing changes, then the inevitable result is *death*. The *death* stage may be an actual end to the business itself or the sale of its assets at less than value just to "get out of the business" or "retire."

The longer you stay on the backside of the curve without that jolt of new life, the harder it will be to turn things around. You can be in any of the stages mentioned above for months, years, or even decades. The key is knowing where your business is and what can be done to move to the next stage on the left side of the curve or rebirth from the peak to the right side of the curve.

> The longer you stay on the backside of the curve without that jolt of new life, the harder it will be to turn things around.

Turning Point

When you are a business owner, you may not be able to see where you are or do anything to change it. If you are an entrepreneur, however, you can and will change. Like the hero of a fiction novel, the E-Hero is the only one who can. So you have to ask yourself, are you a business owner or an E-Hero?

As you continue reading this book, you will see how you can steer your business through the E-Hero's Journey.

Next stop—the danger that comes from without.

The Business Life Curve – Chapter Summary

- **Initial Launch:** You need a business, a name, banking set up, capital to buy supplies and inventory, and possibly a limited liability entity like a Limited Liability Company (LLC). Please reach out to BKM or your business advisor before you launch.
    - When you begin your business, consider some niche industries or markets that you can serve and would enjoy serving.
- **Strategic Growth:** A business coach can guide you through the process of identifying your values and writing down your BHAGs. They will also help you problem-solve when things get tough.
    - Focus on People, Processes, and Systems. You need people who share your values, the process to ensure consistency when you deliver your products, and Systems that enable efficiency and effectiveness.
- **Momentum Growth:** The right people are in the right seats, and it seems nothing can go wrong. Revenues are up, costs are down, and things look great on the surface.

- Growing pains must be minded. Pay attention to the issues of capacity, quality control, responsiveness, and competition.
- **Maturity Phase:** Success involves several factors, starting with the business owner. Do you want to learn and develop? Are you willing to change your methods?
  - This is a business crossroads. You must embrace a new challenge and get new vision or begin to decline.
- **Decline and Death:** The longer you stay on the backside of the curve without that jolt of new life, the harder it will be to turn things around.
- **Turning Point:** You can be in any of these stages for months, years, or even decades. The key is knowing where the business is and what can be done to move to the next stage on the left side of the curve or rebirth from the peak to the right side of the curve.

CHAPTER 9

THE EXTERNAL OBSTACLES

Back to the Matrix, for Neo, the obstacle ahead seemed insurmountable. Impossible even. How could he live up to Morpheus' expectations and take on the agents? Was he even supposed to? Was he "the one"? Neo tried to learn and train for the coming unknown battle, but not until the all-is-lost moment when the agents capture Morpheus does he finally believe.

In every hero's journey, external obstacles like these must be faced for the hero on the inside to manifest on the outside. Clearly, the audience knows the hero of the story. But does the hero know? Not usually. Only when he is tested does Neo take the mantle, arms himself with "guns, lots of guns," and face those obstacles.

Obstacles You Don't See Coming

In the early hours of September 11, 2001, I was on the fifty-sixth floor of the Bank of America building in downtown Dallas. As an auditor for Arthur Andersen, LLP, I was going through the bank reconciliations of a construction business. The day before, we had met the controller at his office and picked up the statements and other records needed to perform our tasks.

The controller didn't know we were hired to check his work and determine if there had been any impropriety on his part. He didn't know he would be fired later the next week and neither did I. We met him while picking up the records. I liked him. He seemed an honest, down-to-earth guy.

While I was going through each line of the bank statements, I noticed a crowd gathering around the televisions mounted on the walls throughout the floor. Andersen was a "virtual office" with open seating for almost all of its employees. Only the partners had permanent spaces, but other staff could use even those if needed. The TVs were in most corners of the office, usually on a news channel.

On that day, everyone stopped working and gathered around the monitors to watch the devastation. In disbelief, we watched the first tower collapse. Shortly after, the building alarms went off. The partners began telling everyone to evacuate. In a silent panic, we all dismissed ourselves down fifty-six flights of stairs.

I didn't say a word. Most of us were quiet as we carefully marched down the stairs. I walked alone to my car, five blocks away, and drove home. On the way home, tears of shock, disbelief, and grief rolled down my face. The days and months following were grim.

A few months later, our firm, accused of wrongdoing on the Enron audit, fought for its existence. It lost. The actions of a handful of people in the Houston office destroyed the livelihoods of sixty thousand employees across the country.

Businesses aren't supposed to end that way. But sometimes, they do end. Devastation like 9/11 and Enron are examples of external obstacles that can disrupt the entrepreneur's journey. In the aftermath of 9/11, many businesses didn't make it. Much like COVID-19 in 2020, obstacles like lockdowns, shortages, and other actions of consumers and the government hurt the small business owner.

What are Obstacles

Obstacles are defined as something in the way or impeding your progress that must be moved or circumvented. Sometimes they seem insurmountable. Most of the time, they are not. They say that you are either leaving a storm, headed into a storm, or in the middle of a storm. Like storms, obstacles in business are inevitable. They will never come at the right time, and they will always pass.

I remember conversing with my wife one night; it was Valentine's day. Our real estate taxes had been due on January 31, and we didn't have the money to pay them. In previous years, if I didn't have the money to pay them, I would borrow against our properties or put them on a credit card. That year, I was determined not to go into more debt for operational expenses. In probably an over-dramatic fashion, I told my wife that we would be bankrupt or God would have to rescue us from the current crisis. It made for an awkward, tense Valentine's dinner.

Before you say that I had gotten myself into that mess, I acknowledge that it was my fault. I didn't prepare as I should have. The amount due at the time was about $40,000. It may as well have been $4 million. We didn't have it. What we did have were some storage units for sale. Unfortunately, they had been for sale for a long time with no interest from any buyers.

Just before the county attorneys filed a lawsuit to foreclose on us, thereby ruining our credit and our potential in real estate, the storage units sold. We had enough to pay off the taxes and fund our savings account with 80% of next year's taxes. I vowed never to leave myself in that position again.

In the next chapter, we will go into the internal conflict that can inflate the obstacles we face. In this chapter, however, I want to focus on the external factors that seem impossible for the new entrepreneur. There are five areas of external forces that can be tremendous obstacles. There are more than these, but we will discuss your most likely barriers. These five areas are:

- Taxes
- Employees
- Customers
- Cash Flow
- Borrowing

We will go over each one in summary to help you. Potential obstacles don't look so big when you understand them and are aware of them. You see them coming down the road and can move or make adjustments to overcome or circumvent them altogether.

Some obstacles have no warning. They come from nowhere to disrupt your business and personal lives. Others, you can prepare for beforehand and ride them through. It is like bad luck versus good luck. Both are events that you don't foresee, but both may provide you with opportunities. It is not the type of luck that determines your success; it is what you do with that luck, good or bad.

Taxes

Taxes are what I do. I understand the fear that can strike when you get a letter from the IRS, sales tax authority, or the like. The best way to overcome this obstacle is by documenting whatever is cost-effective to document.

Clients who don't have good records or a way to retrieve data quickly suffer when an audit letter drops in their mailbox. The worst thing you can do is procrastinate with an IRS letter, especially if you don't have an excellent method of documentation.

I have a client who usually gives me notebook paper with strings of numbers. That was fine when his business was modest, but now his revenue is much larger, and he has substantial transactions. When he got an IRS letter, we recommended that we go back and record his banking and credit card transactions in our accounting software for the last two years. That can be costly and time-consuming. It would have been better if we had been doing it all along, but we got it done.

When we finished, he owed less than what he initially reported. Because we implemented a better documentation process, we identified more deductible expenses than his notebook paper method. Having a good documentation process and an excellent CPA makes an audit less scary.

As an entrepreneur, you will deal with several types of taxes. Federal income taxes (FIT), sales taxes, personal property taxes, payroll taxes, self-employment taxes, real estate taxes, and state income taxes—are all ways the government steals from the entrepreneur. Unfortunately for you, when you don't let the government steal from you, you are the one that is penalized.

You don't have to be an expert at any of these taxing authorities. You just need a partner who will help you navigate the maze of compliance with tax law. Find a specialist in your field. We specialize in the real estate industry. From Realtors to investors, construction companies to mortgage brokers. Therefore, we understand the obstacles they face and can deliver advice specific to them. Somewhere there's a CPA firm that specializes in your industry. Do yourself a favor and find one.

Taxes are an obstacle you prepare for in advance. To do that, you should engage your tax advisor for more than just compliance. That is the lowest value of service they have to offer.

If they don't also offer tax planning, financial planning, and business coaching, you aren't getting all the guidance you need. Compliance records what happened last year. Planning and coaching look at the journey ahead; it sees the roadblocks, potholes, and debris on the road so you can avoid them. You must have a capable tax advisor in your corner for this obstacle.

Employees

Employees can be a source of peace, pride, and satisfaction, or they can be a source of frustration, anxiety, and potential disruption. The good news is that most of the blame for the latter can be placed on your shoulders. Is that good news?

I have even better news—if everything goes well, you definitely do not deserve the credit. When people compliment our firm, my response without hesitation is that I have the best team of accountants, advisors, and administrative staff in the world. I am blessed by how hard they work and what they can accomplish.

When something goes wrong, I don't blame my team (or at least not anymore). The fault is usually mine. I either didn't oversee or failed to create good systems that led to the issue.

You should try to avoid blaming your people when something goes wrong. It doesn't help resolve the problem, and it only discourages your team. Sometimes it can discourage them so much they will not make you aware the next time something goes wrong. You will lose clients and good employees.

Our firm has a blog post on *"The People Question,"* parts one and two. Be sure to read it at www.bkm-cpa.com. In it, I go over when to hire, whom to hire, how you should hire, and what to do when you make a hiring mistake.

Hiring and Firing

The most important thing to remember when hiring is whether or not the candidate holds the company's values. When that's right, everything else is details. Knowing when to hire is determined by your budget, current staff, and upcoming needs.

There are different schools of thought here, but my personal experience puts most of the weight on the budget.

I worked for a church that would make offers to people but at wages substantially less than a living wage. I disagreed with that practice then and still disagree now. If you can't afford someone at a competitive salary, don't make the offer. For many non-profits, people usually feel inspired or "called" to service and may take the low offer because it is in the field where they can use their gifts.

Later they are almost always resentful because they work hard, with little thanks and less compensation.

Also, I don't prefer to manage my employees. Coach, yes; Train, yes, but I absolutely do not want to hold someone's hand or check the clock when they come in. I also don't want to review all their work to ensure it's done professionally or monitor their attire and hygiene. I'm not their mother! When you hire someone who fits your values and the company's vision, you won't have to manage them. Turn them loose and see what amazing things they can do!

> When you hire someone who fits your values and the company's vision, you won't have to manage them.

Terminating someone takes firmness and grace. You can decide to let someone go without tearing into their character. People get laid off for budget or strategic reasons. When the employer can't afford to keep staff, they must release people to keep the business profitable. It sounds harsh, but usually, you save more jobs than you eliminate.

Strategically, you may release staff because the company changed its focus. That department no longer fits with the organization. For example, many CPA firms choose to sell off their individual income tax products to focus on their business tax products. Any tax preparers who aren't trained and may not want to be trained in business returns or planning may need to be cut loose.

I recently had to let go of my remodel crew for our real estate company. It was a challenging day. They hadn't done anything wrong and were very talented. We just didn't need those positions any longer. You never get used to it, but you might ease the pain by paying severance, providing good references, and maybe giving them leads to new jobs.

Firing someone takes the same professionalism and tact as letting someone go. My hope is that those that I have to fire will feel like I was fair, honest, and direct. I haven't always been very good at this part, but like every E-Hero, I am always learning and improving.

Customers

Customers are your boss. Never forget that. That sounds like I agree that the "customer is always right." I don't. Just like my employees expect me, as their boss, to respect them and treat them with dignity, I expect our customers to do the same for my staff. I also expect my firm, myself included, to serve our clients to the best of our ability. One, because that is our mission and purpose, and two, they will fire us if we don't.

Customers can become a source of external obstacles for many reasons. They may not fit with your business model. Maybe they did once, but you have grown, and they have not.

Your fee structure or pricing model may have changed over time, but they don't want to pay the increased cost.

They don't understand that the cost of labor, software, and materials going up means that your prices must also increase. Or maybe they do understand and just don't care. The times where we have had the most conflict with customers had to do with fees or expectations.

When clients don't know the fees upfront, sticker shock can create a massive conflict. Also, a huge conflict results when what the client expects versus what we think they understand for a service or a product is different. The two things happening simultaneously almost always result in losing the client and not getting paid. You need to manage your customer's expectations to avoid losing them.

One way to better understand your customer is to create an avatar of your ideal customer. Give them a name. Maybe one of your current clients fits that description. Ask yourself, "What are their needs, wants, and desires. Why do they pay us? What makes them come to our company?" The answers to these questions will help you understand the customer and better manage their expectations. In addition, you can focus your team's activities on meeting those needs and making them happy.

But you can't make everyone happy. That's an external obstacle completely out of your control.

We recently had a client who had been with us for almost 20 years. Their business had grown out of our expertise and business service model. With reluctance, I called them and told them we couldn't be their CPA firm any longer. I couldn't, in good conscience, take on their projects and promise the level of service they had come to expect. We didn't have the specialized staff to help them. They thanked us for our honesty. We love them and know that they will do so much more in the future. They still call us friends. If we had kept them as clients, both they and our firm would have ended the relationship in frustration. Maybe not immediately, but I could see that it was inevitable.

Cash Flow

Cash flow is the business owner's constant battle in the early days of existence. Remember, you pay your bills with cash! You can't pay them with receivables (money people owe you), nor can you pay them with inventory (money sitting on the shelf waiting to be converted to receivables or cash).

Cash flow is the amount of cash left over each month after all disbursements, including operating expenses and debt service. Sometimes cash is abundant in some months and scarce in others. As a CPA, tax season creates an abundance of cash, but cash is hard to come by during the off-season—the summer months and November and December.

To manage uneven cash flow, you must know your cash requirements during those down months and set aside enough cash to see you through. In addition, you might create a new revenue stream that has different seasons as your primary line of work. For example, many lawn and landscaping companies offer Christmas lighting for your yard and house from October through January. They still have some maintenance for lawn and landscaping, but Christmas lighting gives them additional revenue during the off months.

If you don't have the cash to set aside and don't have the off-season revenue stream yet, you may need to rely on a line of credit with a bank or financial institution. I don't particularly like using a line of credit, but it is available to those with good credit scores and business history. That leads us to the last external obstacle, borrowing.

Borrowing

Applying for and securing a loan can be challenging for many reasons, especially for those just starting on the entrepreneur's journey. Many bank and SBA programs can help. Keep in mind—it sounds dumb saying this, but—whatever you borrow will have to be paid back!

I know how illuminating that was. You're welcome, but when people borrow money for cars, houses, and equipment, they often focus on things *other* than paying the loan back.

You negotiate the best interest rate, find out what you qualify for, and find that thing that will help your business or help you enjoy life. You should be most concerned about how to pay the loan back without shorting your business. If you ever get to a place where you decide what bill to pay and what bill to let float, you have mismanaged your cash flow.

Unfortunately for most, a vacuum effect applies to your cash. For every new dollar earned, an expense pops up to fill the gap. A business should live below its means. Cap your spending at 80% of your earnings; invest 10% and save 10%. It's okay if that takes some time to grow to, but if you don't decide you want to and begin planning how to make that happen, you will never get there.

If you run your business without margin, you become a servant to your lenders. Margin is the space between your revenues and your expenses. Without margin, first, you will reach out to the line of credit we discussed earlier. Then you will max out all of your credit cards. Then you will leverage your equipment, vehicles, and whatever else until you finally go bankrupt.

Borrowing should only be done by the disciplined business owner. If you can avoid borrowing, do so. Start saving to have reserves on hand for emergencies or short months. If you need to borrow, create rules for yourself when borrowing. Set criteria for what you will borrow, how long you should take to pay it back, and should things go wrong, what you are willing to sell to cover the debt.

I will borrow to purchase things that make me money, like houses, trucks, and copy machines. I will also borrow to cover my employees' salaries, not mine. I am willing to finance vehicles for one-third of their useful life, usually around eighteen to thirty-six months. For payroll, it is much shorter. Usually, I want the line of credit paid back by the end of the next quarter. If I can't do that, I need to find another way. I can sell something or do some outside work to make up the difference.

These are by no means all the external obstacles you will face as an E-Hero, but you will face them. Getting familiar with these areas and their nuances in advance will help you navigate the stormy waters. Have a plan before the storm comes. Be prepared. Over and over again, I have said on the podcast, to my staff, and to my kids that reading business books and leadership development books help prepare you for what may come. Of course, you are reading this book, so you are already ahead of most.

I have more good news.

External obstacles are not the limit of what you will face. In fact, these five areas we just discussed may pale in comparison to the five areas of internal conflict we are about to address. But you're an E-Hero, remember? You aren't going to let that stop you! Turn the page, and let's explore the undiscovered territory that is you.

The External Obstacles - Chapter Summary

- External Obstacles will be faced. Knowing this and creating a plan in advance will help you overcome them.
- The five main areas of external obstacles are taxes, employees, customers, cash flow, and borrowing.
- **Taxes**—All entrepreneurs need to engage in tax planning, hopefully with an enlightened CPA who knows your industry. Ideally, you will find a firm that also offers financial planning and business coaching as well.
- **Employees**—When you hire employees, do so with your budget in mind, at a competitive salary, and with employees who share your values.
- **Customers**—Create an avatar of your ideal customer, then ask:
    - What are their needs, wants, and desires?
    - What do they pay me for?
    - Why do they use me and not someone else?

- **Cash Flow**—You pay your bills with cash! Know how much money you need to operate and grow. Manage your uneven cash flow by adding revenue streams or saving.
- **Borrowing**—You must pay back what you borrow. Finding lines of credit can be challenging for new businesses, but this is a better alternative than credit cards. Don't borrow if you can avoid it by selling something else or budgeting to pay cash later.

CHAPTER 10

THE INTERNAL CONFLICT

On the big screen, watching *Star Wars: A New Hope*, you don't know what thoughts bombard Luke's mind. You see his actions, and as the observer through the "fourth wall," you can infer what those thoughts might be. At the beginning of the movie, you can see Luke has dreams of something more, and he presses his uncle about leaving the farm. But later, when Obi-Wan asks him to go on an adventure, his uncle's words come flying out of his mouth. You see the insecurity Luke has within himself at that time.

Later, all of that insecurity goes away. With the strength of "the force" and the words of Obi in his ear, he takes on the Empire to destroy the Death Star.

Every hero has internal conflict.

Your E-Hero journey requires you to grow up in some way. You must be a different person on the other side of the climax. If not, what was it all for? You may have conquered the external obstacles, but if you don't mature and learn something internally, you will only get yourself into the same trouble again.

An employee who had been with me for five years recently decided to take a job at another firm. I was heartbroken. More than that, I was just broken. It had been a difficult tax season, and this news came right in the middle of it. I wrote in my meeting notebook three strategies to deal with this news. One, convince her to stay by giving her raises, benefits, or whatever it would take. Second, hire someone else and begin training when no one has time to train. Third, sell the firm and move to Florida. I leaned pretty heavily towards Florida.

The event took me to a dark place in my mind. I didn't realize it until a friend pointed out that I was going through the five stages of grief. It took time to mourn her loss. I tried my best not to show my other employees how devastating her departure was to me. It started to feel as if the firm was stuck in a never-ending cycle, moving forward a few steps only to stumble further backward, its legs cut and bloodied beneath it.

> You may have conquered the external obstacles, but if you don't mature and learn something internally, you will only get yourself into the same trouble again.

My wife, who has no real love or passion for the firm, wasn't much consolation. I don't blame her. For most of our early married life, the firm took me away from her. Ironically, I had just written a blog on leading through adversity. Let me tell you, those words tested me. Everything I said about managing your emotions and separating the good fear from irrational fear taunted me. All kinds of irrational fear flooded my mind. I had to step back and spend some time alone.

Driving usually helps me to get focused and settle my heart. It gave me a clearer picture of what I needed to do. In hindsight, her resignation was exactly what needed to happen for both her and me. She needed a new firm to find peers with whom she could collaborate. We needed experience in cloud-based client accounting systems. When we found her replacement, we began to improve, and my vision of a Virtual CPA firm was that much closer.

For the E-Hero, internal conflict can come from yourself, others, or circumstances beyond anyone's control. It doesn't matter how you got into the mess. It only matters what happens next. My blog about leading through adversity is on my firm website, www.bkm-cpa.com. I will try not to repeat too much of that blog here, but it may overlap.

The only thing that can keep you from your destiny is you—no outside event, sabotage, loss of an employee, or any competitor's actions can remove the gifts and callings God has given you. You have a choice to move on, rise up, and overcome. You have to make that choice. No one can make it for you.

Emotions and Irrational Fears

To overcome internal conflict, you must get control of your emotions and irrational fears. I am the worst about playing scenarios in my mind about how conversations will go with key contacts or clients. Then when I actually have those conversations, it goes nothing like the fear and anxiety script I had written. In most circumstances, the worst enemy during your entrepreneur journey is you—your mind, your immaturity, your ignorance. Take stock of your self-talk. What do you say to yourself about yourself or about others? Do you think about your thoughts?

Defeatism and victim mentalities have slain many entrepreneurs along their journey. If this were a fiction novel, the inner thoughts and fears would be represented by sickness or poison. Something that can kill but is silent, gaining strength in the darkest corners of your mind.

The inner conflict and doubts of E-Heroes are real. It happens to the newbie just beginning and the seasoned professional who has earned a good living for years. It never goes away. I wish it would. If these thoughts don't attack you regularly, please message me and tell me how you stopped them. But just because a thought comes doesn't mean you have to entertain it. You can remind yourself of how you overcame in the past, or your vision, BHAGS, and mission. This is why early in your journey, I stressed the need for a solid foundation built on the "Why" behind your venture.

My mom used to say, "The road to hell is paved with good intentions!" Likewise, the road to failure is littered with those who refuse to learn and grow as leaders. The only way to overcome this self-doubt and fear is through personal development. There are many books out there written by great authors who have helped others, including me. Check out my "You Should Read" list in the appendix for some of my favorites that helped me understand the interpersonal relationships around my office and with my clients.

Burnout Loop

There have been other times when doubt and fear tempted me to quit. Throughout the years, I had done well in the firm and, at times, had a few staff members. But, around 2007, after trying to add another location and hiring a staff accountant I couldn't afford, I had increased my debt, and it weighed on me. So, when most of the staff had left by attrition, I decided not to hire anyone. It was just me and my bookkeeper, who was also our receptionist.

I began working terrible hours. I made money but had no time for family or fun. I was burning out quickly. This is called the Burnout Loop. You begin to have success and hire more people, but for whatever reason, you have to let people go and take on more of the work. And then it starts again. After a while, it just seemed too overwhelming. I began looking to merge with another firm so that it wouldn't be such a lonely burden. Maybe another firm was overstaffed and had the capacity to handle some of my work?

I am very glad I didn't follow through with that plan. I would not have had near the opportunities or the ability to move into the Virtual CPA firm that I wanted.

Capitulating to a merger would have been a defeat for me. It might have been my pride, but something inside me just would not let me quit. I knew there was potential in my firm, in myself. If I had merged with someone else, I would have had to ask permission to follow my dreams. I couldn't; I wouldn't do that.

So how do you get out of the loop? I can't say that I followed some steps or managed some process. During that time,

I had gone to a financial services conference. On the first day, my wife and I sat across from another CPA at the reception. I talked with him about where I was and how overwhelming it had become. He only offered one piece of advice: Hope is not a strategy.

I couldn't just *hope* things got better. I had to take time to think about my goals. I thought about where the firm started and where it had come. I plotted out all the things that would have to happen to reach my goals. Then, I asked myself what I have asked others since, "Which way forward from here?" I began to focus on just the next step, then the next. All the while keeping in mind my values and priorities. I realized I was violating my most important value: family first.

Even though I "made time" for my kids and my wife by squeezing them in between office hours, I wasn't giving them my whole self during that time.

Burnout happens when you focus on results instead of the process. The ends do not justify the means here. It matters how you get there. It matters that you don't sacrifice the ones you care about for their "provision."

You Are Not Alone

Internal conflicts make us feel alone. One of the biggest lies ever told is that no one else has ever faced that thought or that trial or made that mistake. The best way to combat these thoughts is to have friends and family or business coaches that will walk through it with you. I have had several mentors and what I now know as business coaches, people who challenged me to see things differently. They may not have any experience in the areas I struggled with, but they didn't have to. What they did for me was listen, ask good questions, and help me discover the solution.

Sometimes I can be a bit overdramatic. My kids come by that honestly, I guess. I get so focused and overwhelmed with what I face that the truth hides in the fog of worry and doubt. Talking things out, especially out loud, helps me put things into perspective. It helps delineate between the real and the unreal expectations and consequences. The critical thing to remember is that **you are not alone**.

You might find comfort in reading about other entrepreneurs in business books and biographies. I have listed a few of these in the appendix for you. Reading about others who have been through the same struggles you have is very encouraging. You will glean practical advice from business biographies to overcome those struggles and see how to set up systems and processes that avoid them.

Mission Drift

Another internal conflict also has to do with your values. Sometimes you work in your business for months or even years, and things begin to feel off. You can't put your finger on it, but you know something is wrong. You look into your product, process, and marketing, and it doesn't make sense. You are doing well, or at least okay. What is off?

It could be mission drift.

When you begin to do things out of rhythm instead of on purpose, you can get caught up in the day-to-day operations and completely forget about the "why" behind doing them. It creeps into your business in stages. You may have broken away from one of your values. For instance, I met a client at one of my kid's baseball games to talk about his taxes. I will never do that again. It again violated my important value of family first! I thought it was harmless, but afterward, I realized that it could open the door to blurred lines between work time and family time.

Our firm's mission states that we exist to help small businesses and individuals in our community earn more and keep more of what they earn. It doesn't say anything about preparing tax returns. Yet, for a few years, we did nothing *but* prepare tax returns. We received the clients' source documents, pumped out the tax return, and received compensation. There was no relationship or process to engage with the client in tax planning or business advisory services. It is no wonder many accountants suffer burnout and leave public accounting after a few years. Who wants to be a return factory? We still prepare tax returns, but it is the lowest value service we offer and is only the entry point of our client relationships.

To stay on mission, we must see the big picture even in the low-value services. When you discover how far you have gotten off course, you must make drastic changes to redirect. Making a change falls into the "easier said than done" category. But it can be done. Go back to *The Four Obsessions of an Extraordinary Executive*. Build a cohesive team, get clarity, communicate clarity, and reinforce clarity! The larger the ship, the slower it turns, but it *will* turn.

Managing Change

Internal conflict can also mean conflict within an organization. Sometimes internal conflict arises from the challenges of merging two unique and separate teams and trying to make them one. Most people have difficulty managing change.

In a merger or acquisition, internal conflict within the organization and its management comes quickly. The company's internal conflict soon becomes your internal conflict. New team members may still align with the old vision, or maybe neither new nor old team members even have a vision.

You must manage the change before, during, and after the transition into one company. CEOs second guess themselves, and employees question if it is worth it to stay. Like blended families, each group has a way of doing things, and each thinks their way is best. If the transition is not managed well, the company could lose customers or great employees.

A Texas chain of convenience stores had done well. It had slow and steady growth for years and had hundreds of stores across West Texas. About two-thirds into its history, the original owner sold out to their management team. Because the former owner had groomed them, they maintained and even surpassed what he had done. Then, after several years of success, someone made them an offer they couldn't refuse.

Another convenient store chain bought them out and made millionaires out of everyone on the management team and several long-term employees through the Employee Stock Ownership Plan (ESOP).

Since then, however, the stores have fallen from their former glory by huge margins. I used to work at one of the stores while I was in college. The original owner had set cleanliness standards very high. One of his values insisted that his wife would be perfectly content to use the restroom at any store they owned. We had to clean the bathrooms or check their status every half hour. Unfortunately, the new owners did not have that value or put processes in place to reinforce it.

Now, I wouldn't stop at one of those stores for anything but gas. Why? Because my wife won't use their restrooms. It seems like a simple and petty thing. But what do customers do after they use the facilities? They buy something. Sometimes a lot of somethings. It is better to see if the vision and values of merging or acquiring firms align before the purchase rather than after.

Processes and systems are much easier to align than vision and values. The acquiring firm may lose several of the acquired company's staff, maybe on purpose. It would be better for them to emphasize the vision and values of the company from the start to help integrate the teams together. To avoid internal conflict, the organization should emphasize vision and values to create an atmosphere where anyone from either company may choose to leave if they can't align themselves with the stated vision, mission, values, and BHAGs.

Managing change is the only way for transitions to be successful and reduce the organization's internal conflict

It Came To Pass

These internal conflicts can be overcome. It takes time, patience, and resolve. This reminds me of some of my favorite words from the Bible, "… and it came to pass." It is found in several places, so I won't give the address, but those words speak to me.

The trouble, the insurmountable obstacles, and the inner conflict will pass! It is not a collapsed bridge; it is merely a detour.

The most important thing about all these storms, internal or external, is that we learn from them. Keep failure in perspective.

I have been involved with martial arts since I was fifteen years old. Currently, the organization that I am a part of has tournaments several times during the year all over the U.S. During the matches, the ring judges echo this phrase repeatedly, "There are no winners and losers; there are only winners and learners." Learning is a form of winning.

With so many repeated attempts to demonstrate a working lightbulb without success, a reporter once asked Thomas Edison how it felt to fail 10,000 times. Edison's famous reply was, "I didn't fail 10,000 times. The lightbulb was an invention with 10,000 steps." If you have that attitude, you will be a successful entrepreneur—an E-Hero—and you will win! We will look at what winning means in the next chapter.

The Internal Conflict - Chapter Summary

- To overcome internal conflict, you must get control of your emotions and irrational fears.
- Internal conflicts make us feel alone. One of the biggest lies ever told is that no one else has ever faced that thought or that trial or made that mistake.
- To combat these thoughts, you need friends and family or business coaches who will walk through it with you. You need people who challenge you to see things differently.
- Delineate between the real and the unreal expectations and consequences.

- Internal conflict occurs when you violate your company or personal values. So know your values. Communicate your values, and measure everything by your values.
- Processes and systems are much easier to align than vision and values. Managing change is the only way for transitions to be successful. Make certain you keep team members focused on your vision, mission, values, and BHAGs.
- When you begin to do things out of rhythm instead of on purpose, you can get caught up in the day-to-day operations and completely forget about the "why" behind doing them. When you discover how far you have gotten off course, you must make drastic changes to redirect. Stay on mission.
- Keep failure in perspective: "There are no winners and losers; there are only winners and learners."

CHAPTER 11

THE WIN

In the hero's journey, the win comes in the third act. It is the book's climax where all the obstacles have been overcome, the hero becomes a better version of himself, and the old world is replaced by the new one. For Neo, the win came when he defeated Agent Smith. For Luke, it came with the destruction of the Death Star (version 1.0). Your E-Hero victory may not be quite as thrilling and dramatic, but the difference from your first act to act three is evident.

On December 22, 2000, I was let go from my first job as an accountant. At the beginning of 2001, I worked a few jobs to make ends meet while I applied for full-time work all over Texas. One of which was Arthur Andersen, and you already know what happened to that job.

Before applying, I talked to my step-grandfather about the application process and what I had asked for as a starting salary. He was an Andersen alumnus and had written a recommendation letter for me. I told him that I wasn't sure how much to put for the amount. I didn't know the Dallas-Fort Worth area and what market salaries were.

In San Angelo, where I lived, starting salaries were extremely low. When I told him what I had requested, he said, "That seems fair and in line with the area." Then he gave me this nugget of wisdom: "Don't worry about the money. You do your best work, serve your employer and the client, and the money will come." He was right. I haven't worried about the money since.

So, what does it mean to win? What is winning for the entrepreneur? Is it Charlie Sheen's definition of "winning"? I don't even know what that is. Does winning equal success? We could argue that it does, that being a successful entrepreneur is winning. But what is your definition of success?

Like my step-grandfather said, don't worry about the money. Success isn't about money. But what is it then? I am simple. Simple definitions have more impact on me than complex ones. I define success as *enjoying what I do while having more than enough to meet my needs and the needs of others*. Let's break that down a bit. "Unpack it," as I have heard so many podcasters and hip radio people say.

Enjoying What You Do

Enjoying what you do doesn't mean that there are never any problems. But we should all enjoy the journey. If you hate what you do, that deprives you in all areas of life. The idea of being stuck in an unsatisfying job or career makes my stomach turn. Sometimes our misery is

> I define success as enjoying what I do while having more than enough to meet my needs and the needs of others.

because our attitude needs to be adjusted, but sometimes it is because we need to find a new career.

We talked about this in the dissatisfaction chapter. Enjoyment is a crucial component of work. For work to be satisfying, you must be productive, actively learn, and have enjoyment. These factors form a triangle that improves performance. Anyone will lose focus and joy if they aren't being productive or actively learning. You aren't motivated to learn if you aren't enjoying the environment or the work and aren't seeing results.

If the work environment does not engage your mind or involve people you enjoy working with or work that is fun, you severely hinder your performance. At the same time, if you improve in one area, the likelihood of the other areas improving goes up as well.

Thinking back to the jobs I have loved, they had all three components. One job I particularly enjoyed was being the executive pastor for a small church. Every day, I learned something new. I could see the church gaining ground and the leadership team growing. It was very challenging with some significant issues that seemed to come out of nowhere.

When the church hired me, the previous executive pastor accused me of trying to take his job. He and his wife, who we thought were our friends, turned on us. Other staff members had very different ideas about the direction of the church and how things should operate and felt that I had no business being the executive pastor.

The senior pastor seemed divided between his role as pastor and the CEO of the charter school he started. That made the staff feel abandoned. They thought I was the Band-Aid fix for the pastor. Since he didn't have time to spend with them, he hired someone to do it. It was one of the most challenging times in my professional life. Yet, I can honestly say I loved being there.

I was still running my other businesses, although I had people in place handling most of the executive decisions. Ultimately, I had to resign from the church. I needed to get back to the businesses we had started, and although it was fun for me, my wife was not having a great time being the wife of an executive pastor. My family always comes first, so it wasn't a hard decision for me.

Another time where productivity, learning, and enjoyment were all firing at once was when I worked for a rental car store for a summer before my junior year of high school. I didn't enjoy cleaning cars that much, but I had gotten the job because a few close friends worked there as well. They were extremely diligent in getting the work done and had a blast doing so. In that case, the environment and the people made the difference.

If you aren't enjoying your work, you may be missing one or two parts to the triangle. Sometimes you can just make attitude adjustments, like looking for the learning moment. Sometimes, you are getting ready for a change.

More Than Enough to Meet Your Needs

Having more than enough to meet your needs depends on where you are in life. When I was young and single, that was very easy. One, I had not tasted the finer things in life and didn't know what I was missing. And two, I didn't have to provide for anyone else but myself.

Now that I am older, a husband of an amazing wife, and a father of four awesome kids, having enough means a bit more. Nothing helps drive a person towards success better than the desire to provide for the people closest to you.

I want my wife and kids to have time with me, fantastic vacations full of great memories, college funding if that is what they want to do, and help to start a business if that is what they want. All these things have less to do with *things* than they have to do with becoming what they are supposed to become.

My family is very close, and I love that closeness. But they all know what drives me is being able to provide. Even when sometimes they don't ask or even want my help. I do what I do so that I am able to help if the need arises.

At what point do you have more than enough to meet your needs? That depends on your budget, goals, and personal vision for your family. When you don't have those things written down, you may never get to the *more than enough* position in life.

You might get a raise and then go buy a new car. Or get a large tax refund and buy a motorcycle. Houses, cars, boats, and jetskis all seduce people into additional monthly debt payments. Then, more than enough gets harder and harder to reach.

When you have a vision and a budget, you can discipline your spending and reach that place of abundance.

Meeting the Needs of Others

Meeting the needs of others is the best use of wealth. Giving to a cause, giving to your church, or specific needs of people in your community can't happen if you don't have more than enough to meet your needs.

It doesn't mean that you have to be a millionaire to help those in your community. It does mean that you can't be generous with money that you don't have. I know that some governments do just that, but we are not the government. To give, you must have money to give.

Sometimes people misunderstand giving and think that they are giving to get, that there is some slot machine in heaven that they are putting money into for a big payout. That is not how giving works, no matter what book you ascribe to as holy.

The benefits of a generous lifestyle are better described in a sowing and reaping principle—doing good returns to you. That has been my experience. Our motivation, however, is always to do good because it is good.

I have been a giver since my first job at 14. When I was in college and money was scarce, I did some dumb things with money. I gave the church money that belonged to the utility companies. Then, when I couldn't pay the utilities, I called my pastor for help. I didn't have anywhere else to turn. My wife and I were desperate. The pastor asked if we had been spending wisely. I learned then that giving comes from abundance, not while you are in need.

Tithing is a practice found in the Bible that represents an understanding of the source of your blessings. It returns to God the first 10% of your earnings to honor Him. Giving comes from the abundance you receive from your faithful stewardship.

Trust God to make the work of your hands prosper. And when it does, you have the privilege and duty to give to Him and those around you.

Meeting the needs of others also meets the needs of your soul. It feels good. It brings joy to the receiver and the giver.

Building Something That Lasts

Outside of my definition of success, there is also an inward drive to build something that outlasts me. I passed "more than enough" a long time ago. My CPA firm is doing well, the financial services firm is doing outstanding, and our real estate company is growing.

What compels me to drive forward and accomplish more? The challenge motivates me. It isn't easy to run a business, much less three of them. I love to see people develop into leaders and experts in their fields. My job is to help people become the best version of themselves. What higher calling is there than that? Aside from the Great Commission, there isn't one.

Building a business is really about building people. When you value people—truly value, love, and appreciate people—you see that serving clients and employees are two sides of the same coin. So, winning has all of these components for me. But there are other aspects to winning or having a "win" within the course of business.

> When you value people—truly value, love, and appreciate people—you see that serving clients and employees are two sides of the same coin."

What is Winning?

Some people have a very limited definition of winning. They judge winning based on whether they have met their goal or goals. Goal reached? If not, then you haven't won. If yes, then you have won. Do you want to keep playing? Most people would not want to continue under those terms. That is why it is vital to have incremental goals.

I love having a vision for the future and setting big hairy audacious goals, but you need to have some interim goals along the way. Also, to measure progress towards your goals, you need to track key performance indicators (KPIs). These help measure growth and trends along the way.

Celebrating the small victories along the way will keep you and your team interested in continuing to play. Those KPIs can help with marking incremental successes.

We had a goal of $1 million in revenue for the CPA firm in three years. After the first year, we had moved to 70% of that goal. That is a small victory. After the second year, we had moved to within 87% of the target. Again, we celebrated that win on the way towards our big goal, trending in the right direction!

At that point, we decided to set another goal of $3 million in annual revenue in seven years. Do you see how the KPIs help you stay on target with your main goals? We set other KPIs that were not directly related to annual sales, but when we measured and focused on them, more sales were the result.

If you define what success means to you and develop key performance indicators to help you stay focused on your goals, you have already begun to win. Defining success helps you manage your expectations, and managing your KPIs helps you meet your goals.

Celebrating the small victories keeps your business life in perspective. As an entrepreneur, I have sometimes been so focused on the end goal that I forgot to acknowledge the short-term wins with my staff. It is a huge mistake to do so. But you won't do that because you are a Hero Entrepreneur!

As you get closer to meeting your goals, the company pushes on that flywheel, builds momentum, and turns on its own. It's time to sit back and let the big wheel keep on turning! Or is it? Success brings its own set of challenges. In the next chapter, we'll look at a few of those pitfalls to help you avoid them.

The Win - Chapter Summary

- Success is *enjoying what you do while having more than enough to meet your needs and the needs of others.*
- For work to be satisfying, you must be productive, actively learn, and have enjoyment.
- If the work environment does not engage your mind or involve people you enjoy working with or work that is fun, you severely hinder your performance.
- Having more than enough to meet your needs depends on where you are in life.
- When you have a vision and a budget, you can discipline your spending and reach that place of abundance.
- Giving to a cause, your church, or the specific needs of people in your community can't happen

if you don't have more than enough to meet your needs.
- The benefits of a generous lifestyle can be seen in the principle of sowing and reaping. Doing good returns to you. Meeting the needs of others also meets the needs of your soul. It feels good. It brings joy to the receiver and the giver.
- Building a business is really about building people. When you value, love, and appreciate people, you see that serving clients and employees are two sides of the same coin.
- To measure progress towards your goals, you need to track key performance indicators (KPIs). These help measure growth and trends along the way.
- Celebrating the small victories along the way will keep you and your team interested in continuing to play.

CHAPTER 12

THE PITFALLS OF SUCCESS

Many of our favorite works of fiction have far too much story to be contained in a single volume. So, they become a series. Just when it looks like the hero has triumphed, a new crisis occurs. Or, as we reach the climax of the first book, we learn it was just the beginning of a longer quest. In *The Matrix*, Neo learns the purpose of the *one* and the impending war with the machines. The fate of Zion depends on him carrying the mantle of the *one* into the next movie.

In *Star Wars, A New Hope,* Luke enjoys early success, then joins the rebellion and continues fighting the Empire. After a near-death experience with a bear-like creature, he discovers his next journey begins on the planet Dagobah where he will learn from the aging Jedi master, Yoda.

As an E-Hero, success will bring new challenges and sometimes hide problems that you can't easily see. These pitfalls of success happen to small businesses as well as Fortune 500 companies. No matter who you are, when success comes, be watchful, attentive, and diligent about what got you there.

When my financial services revenues took off, they literally multiplied by twenty-five times in one year; it was a rush. My hard work and patience had paid off. In the following years, I didn't realize the decline in my CPA firm's revenues. We had the normal attrition of clients leaving without replacing those clients with new ones.

Also, I didn't see the strain occurring with my property manager trying to keep up with the maintenance of our real estate holdings. It was three years later before that issue finally revealed itself. I'm thankful that it didn't take as long for me to see the problems with the CPA firm.

Aside from the attrition issues, I also began to behave in ways contrary to who I was. I made decisions differently—hastily, flippantly. The excess cash led me to believe that I was incapable of failure. I bought a new office building with more office space, even though I didn't need the extra space. I hired additional "sales" staff and administrative staff. The sales staff didn't sell anything, and the extra administrative staff was redundant.

The worst part was that no one counseled or advised me—make that, I didn't seek out any counsel or advice. Why would I need anyone else's input? I was the successful genius that accomplished all of this?

Man, I behaved stupidly.

Thankfully, I have a habit of reading a few books repeatedly. One of those is the *Millionaire Next Door: The Surprising Secrets of America's Wealthy* by Dr. Thomas Stanley. When I re-read this book for the seventh time, I realized that I had strayed away from the investing and business habits that had led me to become a millionaire even before the financial services income had made us flush with cash.

I wish I could go back to that time and slap myself to keep me from making those rookie mistakes. But none of us can do that except for Barry Allen, also known as *The Flash*.

The Deception of Pride

The beginning of the end for most successful businesses is *pride*. Or *hubris*, as Jim Collins puts it in *How the Mighty Fall: And Why Some Companies Never Give In*.

When the momentum builds and your company moves forward at lightning speed, it almost seems like you can do no wrong. The underlying truth is that success hides problems. In the beginning, you approached things like a physician to diagnose and eliminate diseased parts of your business. You combed through your P&Ls (Profit and Loss Statements) and checked every expense for its necessity.

It isn't during those times that problems sneak in. Problems sneak in when there's an abundance of customers, cash, and opportunities. That's when the issues find their way in from the shadows. It is almost like success hides the imperfections in the process like a blanket. Success can create a euphoria that blinds you. You feel insulated from failure, so you take your eye off the details.

> The underlying truth is that success hides problems.

The Folly of Fear

Success also creates fear. Some have said that fear can make a person strive for wealth, and then when they get there, it can make them afraid to lose it all. Some of that fear influenced me as well. The financial services income was only from a handful of clients, so I was afraid of losing those clients. I hired more sales staff to increase my book of business so that it wasn't dependent on such a small number of accounts.

Have you ever been in a baseball game where the team on the field playing defense makes a mistake? Not a huge mistake but one that had negative consequences? Maybe a run scored or someone advanced to second base (commonly known as "scoring position"). Then, the next pitch or play, another mistake happens, then another and another.

It's hard to watch, especially at the high school or youth sports level, when the players on the field are your kids. I coached little league for six years. One year, one of the coaches told the players, "Don't respond to one mistake with another one. Calm yourself, breathe, know where you are going with the ball, and make the right play."

That's good advice.

After someone makes an error, fear and doubt get into the players' heads. Nobody wants to be the next person to screw up. So they overthink and can't seem to get their bodies to respond properly. They over grip the ball when they throw it, causing a wild throw. Or they take their eyes off the ball before it lands safely in their glove. Or even worse, they forget how many outs there are.

That's what fear can do to you in business. It can keep you from pursuing opportunities or changing your methods to adapt to the current market. In my case, it meant that I spent this newfound cash in fear of losing that revenue stream. There wasn't any evidence that I would lose that revenue stream. That revenue depended on how well I served those clients. I should have concentrated on serving them instead of my irrational fear. I did serve them, but the fear lingered on my mind.

Ironically, none of the activities I pursued to increase my book of business worked. They all sputtered and failed. The billboards, radio ads, sales staff, etc., all bombed. So how did I turn things around?

Thankfully, I had a moment of clarity. Like that wise coach said, "Calm yourself, breathe, and think about where you are going with the ball if it comes to you."

I thought about how we earned the financial services business in the first place. The answer was serving them with exceptional tax services with the CPA firm. Whenever we focus on the CPA firm, all the other businesses grow. So that is what we did, and the financial services business increased.

We didn't market BKM Financial, LLC. It wasn't necessary. We now train our CPA firm staff on how to see opportunities with our clients to serve them with financial products or services. They now refer the client to one of our financial advisors or myself. This plan has performed very well. It allows us to focus our efforts and keeps the fear of losing financial service clients at bay.

The Stronghold of Vanity

Unwillingness to change methods creates another pitfall to success. This is the "we have always done it this way" mentality. I'm going to call this pitfall the stronghold of vanity. To think that there is no better way to do things is just vanity.

After I graduated college as an undergrad, my first job was with a CPA named Van Carson. He was a solo practitioner who prepared all tax returns by hand. In addition, he performed all bookkeeping engagements on thirteen-column green ledger paper. Cash journals were prepared each month, and then the summations of each category were posted, by hand, to the general ledger—an actual ledger book.

When did I graduate from college? Was it in the 1960s? No. I graduated with a bachelor of business administration from Angelo State University on May 12, 2000. It's hard to believe, but it is true. The computers in the office only created depreciation schedules and tracked long-lived assets.

Once completed by hand in number two pencil, Mr. Carson reviewed the tax returns. He would place an X by any incorrect line in pencil—no explanation for why it was wrong, just an X. The IRS forms indicate that all numbers on Form 1040 and the supporting schedules should be rounded to the nearest dollar.

Mr. Carson only accepted work from me rounded to the penny, or hundredths decimal place. Once, I received a return back with a few Xs on it. I asked what was wrong with the numbers. He said they were off by thirty-five cents (or something like that; I can't remember exactly). Since the initial error occurred on Schedule C or E, or F, that meant I had to change not just Form 1040, but at least four forms and schedules all required recalculation.

If a return passed muster, it was sent to a "typist" to convey the penciled numbers onto blank forms printed from the IRS website. Why am I telling you this? To share my pain with the world, of course! And to say that Van Carson did things the same way his father, also a CPA, had done. With slight changes in their methods in over 50 years, you have to ask why?

Was it better for their clients?

No, it took way too long to process. Hours of work were applied to a return, with a ton of potential for errors, all billed to the client.

So what besides fear of change kept this office frozen in time? Simply put, his dad had success doing things that way. Why bother changing when you know what works, right? This stronghold of vanity is rooted in not understanding the difference between *vision*, *strategy*, and *tactics*.

Vision includes your values, which never change. It also includes your mission, which rarely changes. The mission may be tweaked here and there as your purpose evolves over time. Lastly, it includes your Big Hairy Audacious Goals (BHAGs). These only change once accomplished. So vision, mission, and goals are the constant.

> This stronghold of vanity is rooted in not understanding the difference between *vision, strategy, and tactics.*

The strategies and tactics used to achieve the mission and goals can and should change. Specifically when disruptive technology has become available or the client has adapted to a different service model. Strategies and tactics must be flexible.

Can you guess that Mr. Carson didn't e-file? That is a customer adaptation that should have moved the firm towards tax preparation software. But it didn't. He lost clients and lost revenue because his service model didn't change.

Avoid the Pitfalls of Pride, Fear, and Vanity

So how can you overcome these pitfalls? Pride, fear, vanity? They all happen when you have had a taste of success. Of course, you can experience these without success, but the likelihood increases when the momentum has shifted in your direction.

The key to overcoming these traps is having mechanisms that realign you. Do you remember I said I have a few books I read over and over again? These books, for me, were foundational in helping me find success. Because they helped lead me in the first place, they still have a way of centering me. (You really need to take advantage of my "You Should Read" list in the appendix. It's gold!)

Books are a reliable mechanism, but they don't have to be the only mechanism. Some lean on their faith, and some spouses are particularly good at bringing us back to reality or warning us of trouble ahead.

During World War II, Winston Churchill formed a group that gave him information that no one else would. He did this because his immediate staff tended only to provide him with good news. They told him what they thought he wanted to hear. But Mr. Churchill knew that if they were going to be successful, he needed the cold hard facts.

If you have a leadership team, while still fighting to push the flywheel, create a system or a mechanism within the team that helps keep you informed of potential missteps. Stay approachable. Listen actively. The book of Proverbs in the Bible is an excellent course-correcting handbook. The principles there are timeless.

You might need a combination of mechanisms. I know this will come as a shock, but I can be hard-headed sometimes. I need books, my wife, friends, sometimes a business coach or counselor, and the Holy Spirit speaking for me to hear. I hope you won't need that much intervention in your life, but if you do, I hope you are willing to receive it.

Humility is the beginning of wisdom. Staying teachable and seeking to learn while driving for continuous improvement is the best way to live. Not because of fear, but because your journey is more fulfilling when you value others and value information. I have interviewed a few CEOs, and the successful ones walk humbly.

As you begin to attain success and learn to avoid the pitfalls that go with it, you will, at last, be ready to live The Better Life.

The Pitfalls of Success - Chapter Summary

- The beginning of the end for most successful businesses is *pride* or *hubris*.
- Success hides problems. Problems find their way in from the shadows when there's an abundance of customers, cash, and opportunities.
- Fear can make a person strive for wealth, and then when they get there, it can make them afraid to lose it all.
- Unwillingness to change methods creates another pitfall to success, the stronghold of vanity.
- The stronghold of vanity is rooted in not understanding the difference between **vision** (the

constant) and **strategy and tactics** (the flexible, adaptable means of achieving the vision).
- The key to overcoming these three pitfalls—pride, fear, and vanity—is to have mechanisms in place that realign you.
- Sometimes you might need a combination of mechanisms like books, your spouse, friends, a business coach or counselor, and the Holy Spirit.
- Humility is the beginning of wisdom. Staying teachable and seeking to learn while driving for continuous improvement is the best way to avoid the pitfalls of success.

CHAPTER 13

THE BETTER LIFE

Remember life in Act One of your E-Hero journey? Well, Act Three looks a **lot** different! Now you know you are a hero. You've got some adventure behind you, and you behave and live differently than when you first started out.

Let's revisit our *Star Wars* metaphor. At the end of *A New Hope*, Luke walks with confidence and purpose. He sees his destiny before him, and it energizes him. He no longer runs from a battle but towards it. Cue the music and the cool words scrolling through space across the screen, and we hit the next episode—*The Empire Strikes Back*[4]. Act One of this film picks up where Act Three of the last one left off. Luke is now a trusted friend of the princess and has responsibilities in the rebel army. Luke lives in the world he always dreamed of, the world his uncle tried to shelter him from. He's where he wants to be.

For an E-Hero, the "better life" contains purpose and direction. You finally know why you were put on this earth. Mark Twain once said, "The two greatest days in a man's life are the day

---

4   *The Empire Strikes Back* by George Lucas, released May 21, 1980.

he was born and the day he finds out why!" The why was there all along, but it takes the journey, the adventure, to discover it.

Any life with passion is better than a life without it! That falls under the "give me liberty or give me death" section of quotes you can take to the bank. The life of an E-Hero ignites the passion inside you. At least the life I am writing about in this book. I know I have said this before, but if you hate your job, ***find something else!***

> Any life with passion is better than a life without it!

Once you have come up with a few ideas, make the choice! I promise it is worth it to face the obstacles in your path and press toward your goal. You can do it! You have everything you need in between your ears and in your heart! Starting a business brings value to your community, your working life, and yourself.

What would be a better life for you? What does success mean to you? Leaving the world a better place? Financial independence? As a hero entrepreneur, it's all possible. Having met with and counseled hundreds of business owners in my life and career, all of them share this: They would not trade their life with any other!

One of my friends started a lawn business at the age of 17. He saw the value of being his own boss then and has never looked back. He now charges the wealthiest clients in the most affluent neighborhoods thousands of dollars to landscape and maintain their yards and gardens. With several employees working for him, he enjoys this better life with his family.

There are thousands of stories like this in books and podcasts all over Spotify and Amazon's bestseller list. Movies and

TV tend to portray the small business owner as constantly struggling with no real joy at work. And they absolutely hate the big business owners or executives.

They present most CEOs as selfish or evil. It is no wonder that most of today's under thirty-year-olds don't even think about a career in business or owning a business. You must break through all the messages you receive in school that you must work in government or for some non-profit organization to do something meaningful.

Social Value of Business

Business has social value. It is the best form of revitalization and rehabilitation for any neighborhood, city, or region. When a man or a woman can start a business with little or no interference from their government, they will satisfy a need and serve their local community. As they profit, they hire employees and help their economic status. It is a win/win scenario.

In addition, most local businesses donate to youth sports, their chamber of commerce, and local charities that also serve the community. One of the business owners I interviewed on my podcast, *Coaching for Profit,* talked about their company's "Bigger Purpose." The company employs its *bigger purpose* to give to its community in ways that its staff is passionate about.

Each year or quarter, the *bigger purpose* committee meets to decide what charities they will contribute to and how they will raise the money among their staff. Sometimes the fundraising becomes a competition between the eight locations of the company. It engages their team and helps every level of employee know that what they do serves that *bigger purpose*.

If you want to do more than just exist in life, start a business. If you want to change your world, start a business!

Personal Fulfillment

While in the dissatisfaction stage, you are susceptible to all the whims and directives of your employer. They may not share your values or capture your heart with their mission, but it was a job.

Jobs are important. All jobs are important. I want to stress that so you know how much I respect every job, and every employee who gets out of bed puts on their uniform or work clothes and gets things done. The difference that I am drawing attention to is the employee's *attitude* about that job.

As an employee, are you fulfilled? Are your values the same as your employer's? Do you see your job as a calling or a means to support your calling? That's just as fulfilling as the person who sees their job *as* their calling. They push that broom because their service funds their kid's education or the mission in Costa Rica to educate girls in small villages.

The point is that what job you do doesn't matter as much as your attitude and how dislocated you feel there. If you have a good attitude but still feel like you should be doing something else, that is the time to evaluate making a move and counting the costs.

The opposite of dissatisfaction is satisfaction. Mind-blowing stuff here. If you have ever taken a survey, you have been asked this question: "Are you Very Dissatisfied, Dissatisfied, Neutral, Satisfied or Very Satisfied?" Have you ever asked that question about your career? Having job satisfaction doesn't mean you don't have issues at work. In fact, the problems at work could be what excites you on the job.

For problem-solvers like me, if there isn't a problem, then why am I there? Challenges are what make work worthwhile. If you aren't challenged, you won't be satisfied. A hero entrepreneur must solve problems. The products and services that we sell have to solve a problem or meet a need of our customers.

The joy felt when you see your products and services meet those needs cannot be understated. It is an amazing feeling. The fact that people will pay you to meet those needs magnifies that feeling. That is what I mean by being a hero entrepreneur! When you have a great product or service, even having just a good product or service that you do with excellence, it makes you the hero in someone's life.

> The products and services that we sell have to solve a problem or meet a need of our customers.

Being the Hero Entrepreneur

I had a squirrel problem. Those little rodents with fluffy tails were getting into our house and playing around in our attic. They had chewed holes here and there, and I didn't know what to do. I called a local vendor, and they made an appointment, inspected our property, and gave us a game plan to correct the problem.

They not only removed the squirrels but made repairs to our house and made sure that they couldn't get back in. They saved us from the rats with furry tails and the snakes who love them infiltrating my attic, and they received financial compensation as my thank you.

What does being a hero entrepreneur do for you as an individual? After each external obstacle and internal conflict you face, you grow as a leader. When I began in business, I had some very rough edges. I was short with people and lost my temper often. I would take it personally when clients left, even for neutral reasons.

I had a client leave because their cousin or other family member became a CPA. I didn't take it well and told them I thought it was a mistake. I was probably right, but I have learned that it is best not to burn bridges. If they want to try someone else, I will bend over backward to help them with the transition. After more than twenty years in the firm, I have seen people leave and come back multiple times. Why? Because I didn't burn the bridge, I did not take it personally and served them until the end.

My family and friends are grateful for my personal growth. My wife and kids especially have seen a difference in how I interact with them. I will read several books per year—usually twenty to forty or so. From each, I learn how to be a better salesperson, team leader, or communicator. It never fails, though, that I will read something and think back to a discussion with my wife or kids and realize how I could have handled it better.

Sometimes, I read books on relationships to develop better relationships with my staff and clients. But I would be foolish not to integrate what I have learned into my close relationships. Books like *Necessary Endings* by Dr. Henry Cloud helped me understand the boundaries I need to place in my life for my family's sake. It also helped me understand some of my client's behavior.

I don't see my business life and personal life as two separate existences. I am one person without split personalities. I want to be the same person in private that I am in public. An entrepreneur's business pursuits will help them be better spouses, parents, siblings ... I say this knowing that there are many examples of business owners behaving badly and who wrecked all those relationships in the course of running a business.

That has more to do with the choices of those business owners. You choose to learn lessons and apply them to your family life, or you don't. For every business owner who behaves poorly, I can find ten who behave with integrity and honor. If you are teachable and look for the lessons, you will find them.

What is The Better Life?

So what is the better life? Whether you define it as benefiting your community, enhancing your working life satisfaction, or the goal of continuous self-improvement, the E-Hero's Journey can get you there. I want to stress that being self-employed is not for everyone. Releasing the entrepreneurial spirit, on the other hand, is for everyone.

You can be an E-Hero employee! It is up to you, and it is within you to be the best you. Do you believe all this talk about business, leadership development, personal development, giving back to the community, and providing for your family, all while increasing your enjoyment at work and personal satisfaction? Don't take my word for it. Go find some entrepreneurs who inspire you and ask them?

Ask about their challenges and how they overcame them. Ask about what is most important to them and how that channels their behavior at work. Ask about their daily routines and what motivates them.

Just Pull the Trigger

Before investing in real estate, I asked a friend who had twenty-six properties how he got started. It spurred a two to three-year conversation about real estate, property management, and the real estate market. This guy was one of the pastors at our church. He was cool. We called him the *Indiana Jones* of the mission field. He went all over the world for the ministry, smuggling Bibles and Christian literature into countries where that could cost you your freedom or even your life!

The church didn't pay much of his way, so he invested in real estate to make up the difference and became a Realtor. Finally, after listening and patiently answering my dumb questions (yes, they do exist), he said, "Brandon, at some point, you're going to have to just pull the trigger!" So I did. I bought my first house and then my second, and then after a few years, I had twenty-six houses, then fifty, then over 100.

At some point, you will have to pull the trigger. It may not mean changing jobs or quitting your job to start a business. It may mean changing your attitude at your current job. The next step for you might be exploring the possibility of a franchise.

Today, at a business connector meeting, I heard about a woman and her husband buying property near the Dallas/Fort Worth, Texas metroplex and starting a cage-less dog kennel and dog sitting service. They didn't quit their jobs at first, but they had to as the referrals kept coming.

> Don't wait on things to change, eventually. Make the choice, go on the adventure that changes you on the inside and out.

Sometimes pulling the trigger works like that. A side hustle that turns into your full-time hustle. Sometimes you have to jump in with both feet. You get to decide. You choose your destiny! Don't wait on things to change, eventually. Make the choice, go on the adventure that changes you on the inside and out. Become the hero of your story. Become an E-Hero!

The Better Life - Chapter Summary

- If you want to do more than just exist in life, start a business. If you want to change your world, start a business!
- Not every E-Hero owns a business. Do you see your job as a calling or a means to support your calling? As an E-Hero employee, that's just as fulfilling as the person who sees their job as their calling.
- Challenges are what make work worthwhile. If you aren't challenged, you won't be satisfied.
- An E-Hero must solve problems. The products and services you sell have to solve a problem or meet your customers' needs.
- An E-Hero's business pursuits will help them be better spouses, parents, siblings ...
- Whether you define "the better life" as your business benefiting your community, enhancing your working life satisfaction, or the goal of continuous self-improvement, the E-Hero's Journey can get you there.

CHAPTER 14

THE CONCLUSION

Wow! What a journey! As an E-Hero, you have been through a lot or will be if you haven't yet chosen this life. Maybe this book is the catalyst that throws you out of your normal, everyday life and compels you to seek something else? But why? Why would you do something so risky, so full of pitfalls and trials? You know the answer—it's all for the better life. And, it really is a better life.

In 2013, sometime around Thanksgiving, my wife's dad called a family meeting. Larry wasn't just my father-in-law; he was one of my best friends. We spent a lot of time together, fishing and working on properties. My wife's family has always been very close, and for several years we all lived on the same street in San Angelo, Texas. When I say all of us, I mean my family of six, my wife's sister's family of five, and then Memaw and Pa. (That was what our kids called Larry and Beth, my in-laws.)

Larry had worked for a grocery store for thirty-plus years. He was tall and strong. He never lifted weights at a gym, but as the grocery store's produce manager, you lift fifty-pound crates of bananas, apples, and other perishables every day. His muscular stature wasn't his greatest strength, however. His greatest strength was his ability to love people.

We really couldn't take him anywhere without him spending time talking with the people around him. Since he worked at the grocery store, that was his home turf. He couldn't help saying hello to other employees or strangers that looked like they needed prayer. My wife would say that sometimes they would send him in to get one thing, and thirty minutes later, he would emerge. Sometimes without the thing he went in for.

That family meeting was one of the worst days of my life. All of us gathered around as Larry told us he had been diagnosed with cancer. The doctors only gave him a few weeks or possibly months. Most of us stared in disbelief at what we were hearing. Because Larry loved Jesus and he knew Heaven was his home, he was ready. None of the rest of us were. He began to lose weight over the next few weeks, and the disease started to take over.

Larry seemed to keep hanging on, not because he wanted to stay but because he was concerned about the welfare of his family. Angela, my wife, spoke to him about our kids. She let him know they would all miss him, but they would be fine.

As an employee of a small grocery store, Larry didn't have much saved up for himself and his wife to live in retirement. The stores he worked for had changed hands multiple times in those 30 years. Each time they required him to roll over his 401k or receive a distribution.

Even with the tax consequences, Larry would take the distribution. He used it to pay off credit cards or give to the church or others in need. When he quit the grocery business, he had about six thousand dollars left in his 401k account.

He and I decided to form a partnership to buy real estate. He used some equity in a piece of real estate he had inherited, and I used my market knowledge to buy several properties. At this time and after our partnership had changed a bit, he had about nine properties that cash-flowed around two thousand dollars per month. It was modest, but it was better than his retirement accounts could do.

He enjoyed working on the properties, and Beth managed the money. Later, he took a job pushing "dirt" around at the city waste treatment plant. The job paid well enough and had a pension after five years. So when this meeting occurred, he was better off financially than he had ever been. But when I met with him during his final days on this earth, I felt like he was still concerned about Beth's financial well-being. He couldn't speak at this point, so I don't know if it was the case.

When I sat in the room with him, he struggled to breathe. I told him, "You don't need to worry, Pa. I know you are concerned about what Beth will do now. I will take care of all of her financial needs. She will never want for anything."

As I have mentioned before, 2013 was a windfall year for us. I can see now that it wasn't just for us. It was for them. For Memaw and Pa. If I had followed the familiar "get a good job" path like everyone else did, I wouldn't have been confident in making that statement. Of course, I would have done my best to be there for them, but now, I can care for her from the overflow of my entrepreneurial journey.

Summary Of The E-Hero's Journey

I wrote this book to inspire you to take that step, get out of your comfort zone, and become that E-Hero.

We talked about what an entrepreneur is and what sets them apart, both as self-employed individuals or team members as employees. The entrepreneurial spirit stirs a person to do great things, to be a better person, business owner, or employee.

We also discovered the **dissatisfaction** that happens in every entrepreneur's life. That feeling that won't go away, the voice that says, "This can't be all there is!" This stirring that leads to change is more of an awakening than just dissatisfaction. Some of that dissatisfaction is seeing needs around you and having no resources to help.

Like with my in-laws, this life adds value to those around you. It opens the E-Hero's eyes to what is possible. That's when the **ideas** start to flow, and plans start to evolve.

We discussed **the choice** to develop these ideas and counting the costs. We also warned against telling your dreams to dream stealers. There is danger in telling people who have never done anything, people who want to hold you back. You want advisors, mentors, and coaches, but you need to avoid the negativity that can shoot you down before you even take flight.

> When you have the right voices in your head, those who speak faith, hope, and love, you can do what God put in your heart to do.

When you have the right voices in your head, those who speak faith, hope, and love, you can do what God put in your heart to do. You can answer **the call to lead**. It is impossible to eliminate all the negative voices around you, but you can focus on those that build you up. Those that encourage you and ask good questions that bring you to understanding; those voices are your beacon, your lighthouse in the storms.

We walked through the process of **unleashing your potential** by being a constant learner. You can awake active learning through awareness of your personal responsibilities. Not only should you become self-aware, but then take steps to develop those in your care. You can be the catalyst that unlocks the potential in others! Through this coaching culture, you and your team can be productive, enjoy working together and challenge each other every day!

Then we talked about **the business life curve**. You can determine on your own what stage you are in. Reflecting on the E-Hero's Journey discussed in the preceding chapters, you might ask how the life curve stages interact with the journey. Like the business life curve, you can go through the journey repeatedly. Creating new goals and new vision will create new external obstacles and reveal new internal conflicts.

Generally, there is one overarching saga or storyline in works of fiction, with several smaller storylines happening simultaneously. The hero entrepreneur experiences this as well, especially if they engage in more than one business at a time.

We learned about the **external obstacles** and **internal conflicts** that everyone goes through. You aren't alone! Don't isolate yourself. These things happen to the new business owner and the seasoned professional. It is not the struggle that defines you; it is how you respond. What is on the inside will come out.

You can overcome because you have resources that historically have never been available, like Google and Amazon. I'm not promoting them but using them as an example of how times have changed for business owners. When I started, these organizations didn't exist or were at their infant stage. You also have mentors, coaches, and other business owners around you who can help. Stick close to your team of advisors, and you will get through it.

We talked about what it means to **win**—having more than enough, enjoying the journey! It isn't that difficult to understand. Simple really. Just because it is simple doesn't mean it isn't challenging. Winning is managing expectations within yourself and defining success for you.

One thing that wasn't in the chapter on winning is being content and thankful for where you are in life. An old minister I know said, "I'm not where I want to be, but thank God I'm not where I used to be!" He also said, "It could be worse. I could be in the hospital. I could be in prison. Thank God I'm just in a life struggle!" Your perspective matters.

We mentioned the **pitfalls of success**: pride, fear, and vanity. All three can be the beginning of the end. A wise proverb says, "Pride comes before destruction and a haughty spirit before a fall." It's unnerving how deceptive pride is. You may not even be aware of pride creeping in until it's too late.

Create mechanisms in your life to protect yourself. You need family, friends, and habits that set reminders of how you got to where you are in the first place. If you don't have these things in place, you isolate yourself from reality. The cold hard facts are necessary to make good decisions and stay grounded.

The better life we talked about means freedom; it is enjoying your work and personal development. You will be better off releasing this entrepreneurial spirit rather than just coasting through life or settling for a job you hate.

The better life isn't without struggles, but you will have more joy because of the satisfaction it brings. In addition, this better life makes you better. With you becoming better, your community becomes better, and so on. The value of small businesses and the entrepreneurial spirit cannot be overstated. It is the backbone of our communities.

What Will You Do Next?

So what happens next? Are you going to read this book and take to heart the message? Will it inspire you to make a move towards your own E-Hero Journey? I hope so. Some people work for others their whole lives and have nothing of value to show for it in the end. Others, as employees, save and add to their retirement plans and end up with a modest amount of retirement assets.

But what might be possible if you took the information in this book and purchased an existing business or started your own? You could be setting the foundation for your family legacy. You could create something in your generation that lasts for the next three. I can tell you, though, that what might be possible will never exist if you don't do something. You fail 100% of the times that you don't make an attempt.

As a business coach and CPA, I have been able to help small business entrepreneurs like yourself with their journey. Whether starting with a new product idea, investing in real estate, starting a restaurant, or some online retail store, I would love to see your vision come to fruition.

I wrote this book as a guidebook or a map for the entrepreneur hero traveler. To help you see ahead of your current space and understand what is coming. I hope it will inspire you to get out of your comfort zone and become that E-Hero. To quote a popular home improvement store, "You can do it. We can help!"

Want More?

Listen to the *Coaching For Profit* podcast wherever you enjoy listening to podcasts and don't forget to leave a review or send a comment.

To receive our newsletter, be on our email list for new books, blog posts, or podcasts, or just to send me a comment or ask a question, please connect with me at **www.brandonkmoore.com**.

Journey on, E-Hero!

THE E-HERO'S GUIDE TO
REAL ESTATE INVESTING

Increase Your Cash Flow
Without Increasing Your Work Day

AVAILABLE NOW ON AMAZON.COM

APPENDIX

YOU SHOULD READ LIST

Books On Writing and Publishing:
- Sean Platt and Johnny B. Truant's *The Fiction Formula: The New Rules For Self-Publishing Success*
- *Save the Cat! Writes A Novel: The Last Book on Novel Writing You'll Ever Need*, Jessica Brody based on books by Blake Snyder
- *Write. Publish. Repeat. The No-Luck-Required Guide to Self-Publishing Success*, Sean Platt, Johhny B. Truant with David Wright
- *The Scribe Method: The Best Way to Write and Publish Your Nonfiction Book*, Tucker Max and Zach Obront
- *Marketing Your Mind: Brand Yourself, Write Your Book, Build Your Platform*, Wendy K. Walters

Books on Financial Independence:
- Robert Kiyosaki, *Rich Dad, Poor Dad, What The Rich Teach Their Kids About Money That The Poor Do Not*
- *The Millionaire Next Door: The Surprising Secrets of America's Wealthy* by Dr. Thomas Stanley

Books on Starting and Operating a Business:
- *The E-Myth Revisited: Why Most Small Businesses Don't Work And What To Do About It*, by Michael E. Gerber
- Patrick Lencioni, *The Five Dysfunctions of a Team: A Leadership Fable*
- *The Four Obsessions of an Extraordinary Executive*, Patrick Lencioni
- *Good to Great: Why Some Companies Make The Leap...And Others Don't*, Jim Collins
- Jim Collins and William Lazier, *Beyond Entrepreneurship 2.0: Turning Your Business Into An Enduring Great Company*

Books on Leadership:
- John Maxwell, *Developing the Leaders Around You: How To Help Others Reach Their Full Potential*
- John Maxwell, *Developing the Leader Within You*

- *The Four Obsessions of an Extraordinary Executive*, Patrick Lencioni
- *The Speed of Trust: The One Thing That Changes Everything* by Stephen M. R. Covey with Rebecca R. Merrill
- Patrick Lencioni, *The Five Dysfunctions of a Team: A Leadership Fable*
- Jim Collins, *How the Mighty Fall: And Why Some Companies Never Give In*

Books on Coaching and Performance:

- *The Inner Game of Tennis: The Classic Guide To The Mental Side Of Peak Performance*, W. Timothy Gallwey
- Timothy Galway, *The Inner Game of Work: Focus, Learning, Pleasure, and Mobility in the Workplace*
- *Coaching for Performance: The Principles and Practice of Coaching and Leadership*, Sir John Whitmore

Books on Systems and Process Management:

- *The Goal* by Eliyahu M. Goldratt
- *The E-Myth Revisited: Why Most Small Businesses Don't Work And What To Do About It,* by Michael E. Gerber

Books on Relationships:
- *Necessary Endings*, Dr. Henry Cloud
- *Boundaries: When to Say Yes, How to Say No to Take Control of Your Life*, Dr. Henry Cloud and Dr. John Townsend
- *The Four Laws of Love: Guaranteed Success for Every Married Couple*, Jimmy Evans
- *The 5 Languages of Appreciation in the Workplace: Empowering Organizations by Encouraging People*, Gary D. Chapman, PhD and Paul White, PhD
- *The 5 Love Languages: The Secret to Love That Lasts*, Gary D. Chapman, PhD
- *The Bible*

Books on Real Estate:
- *The Book on Rental Property Investing: How to Create Wealth with Intelligent Buy and Hold Real Estate Investing*, Brandon Turner
- *Retire Early with Real Estate: How Smart Investing Can Help You Escape the 9-to-5 Grind and Do What Matters More*, Chad Carson
- *The E-Hero's Guide to Real Estate Investing: Increase Your Cash Flow Without Increasing Your Workday*, Brandon K. Moore

ABOUT THE AUTHOR

Brandon Moore is a CPA, Certified Wealth Strategist©, coach, and real estate investor who equips others to thrive in reaching their financial goals. Like many successful entrepreneurs, however, Brandon's career path hasn't been direct. The curves in his route have defined his success—while deepening his expertise.

Brandon didn't graduate at the top of his high school class. Instead, he lost his only run at student council, and a bout of pneumonia gave him an early (and perhaps fortuitous) opportunity to drop out of college (without grief from his father, he says).

After working as a janitor, losing a job as a life insurance agent, and serving as church youth director and eventually bookkeeper, Brandon decided to pursue a new career: that of an accountant.

Brandon then graduated from Angelo State University and began investing in real estate—buying and managing over

100 houses. A few years after graduating college, he acquired his CPA designation, and at age thirty-one, bought his first CPA firm—while building his real estate empire. Later, he purchased another four accounting practices. And during the 2008 recession, he acquired his financial service licenses to better serve CPA clients. He passed the Series 7, Series 66, and Life Insurance Agents license tests and has consistently remained in the top five to ten advisors of his broker/dealer.

Today, Brandon advises clients on wealth management—including charitable giving, estate planning, tax planning, retirement planning, investment allocation, risk management, and more. Brandon and his wife of twenty-five years, Angela, invest in and manage single-family properties and duplexes in West Texas. They have four children, who have been involved in the real estate business from early on.

Beyond the certifications and accolades, Brandon believes his purpose is to coach and develop leaders. He wants his family, friends, and clients to become their best selves, which is why he writes books and runs his podcast, "Coaching for Profit." He says, "I may only be able to coach a handful of people per day, week, or month. But these books can reach people exponentially."

In his free time, Brandon loves music and plays multiple instruments—often in his church. Brandon also recently reached his goal of third-degree black belt in Taekwondo, believing that martial arts offer a continuous improvement philosophy—training both mind and body.

Connect with Brandon at www.brandonkmoore.com.

Made in the USA
Columbia, SC
13 February 2024